Lakatos: An Introduction

D0024218

This will be a valuable book for those interested in the philosophy of science. A proper appreciation of Lakatos' unique contribution to both the philosophy of science and the philosophy of mathematics is long overdue. Larvor's work is a perceptive study, and it can only be hoped that it will lead to a better understanding not only of the importance of Lakatos' thinking but also the development and appraisal of his theories.

George S. Botterill, University of Sheffield

Brendan Larvor's *Lakatos: An Introduction* is the first comprehensive analysis of the intellectual life and theories of the distinguished thinker Imre Lakatos. Larvor, in his clear and direct style, argues that Lakatos developed a philosophy of mathematics which stressed the methodological similarities between mathematics and empirical science. The author locates Lakatos in the liberal-rationalist tradition and explains connections between his life, his philosophy, his politics, and his technical work on science and mathematics.

Lakatos: An Introduction is an essential read for both scholars and students of the philosophy of science and mathematics.

Brendan Larvor is a lecturer in philosophy at the University of Hertfordshire.

Lakatos: An Introduction

Brendan Larvor

London and New York

First published 1998
by Routledge
11 New Fetter Lane, London EC4P 4EE

Simultaneously published in the USA and Canada
by Routledge
29 West 35th Street, New York, NY 10001

Typeset in Palatino by Routledge
Printed and bound in Great Britain by Creative Print and Design
(Wales), Ebbw Vale

British Library Cataloguing in Publication Data
A catalogue record for this book is available from the British Library

Library of Congress Cataloging in Publication Data
Larvor, Brendan
Lakatos: an introduction / Brendan Larvor.
p. cm.
Includes bibliographical references and index
1. Science–Philosophy. 2. Mathematics–Philosophy. 3. Lakatos.
Imre. I. Title.
Q175.L277 1998
501–dc21   97–26569

ISBN 0–415–14275–X (hbk)
ISBN 0–415–14276–8 (pbk)

For Sarah

Contents

Acknowledgements

I am grateful to Dr Peter Fehér, Dr Nigel Swain and Professors Robert Evans, György Geréby, Márta Ujvári and Jancis Long, who all commented on drafts of Chapter 1. Dr Richard Ashcroft, Dr Daniel Isaacson, Dr Lewis Griffin, Mr Rupert Ward and Mr Francesco Guala were kind enough to read an entire draft and Dr Michael Inwood provided invaluable comments on my reading of Hegel. I am also indebted to two readers at Routledge whose criticisms helped me to make significant improvements.

Much of the research for this book was done while studying for my DPhil, when I enjoyed the support of my supervisors, Professor Michael Dummett, Dr William Newton-Smith and Dr Daniel Isaacson. Some responsibility for the present work must also lie with my examiners, Dr Timothy Williamson and Dr John Worrall. I first began to read Lakatos at Queen's University, Ontario, and I have not forgotten the support I enjoyed there.

I am grateful to Cambridge University Press for permission to quote from *Criticism and the Growth of Knowledge*; to the British Library of Political and Economic Science for permission to cite correspondence held in the archives there; and to the editor of the *British Journal for the Philosophy of Science* for permission to quote from Lakatos' original *Proofs and Refutations* essay.

Abbreviations

Works by Lakatos:

Thesis *Essays in the Logic of Mathematical Discovery*, PhD thesis, Cambridge, 1961.

P&R *Proofs and Refutations*, J. Worrall and E. Zahar (eds), Cambridge: Cambridge University Press, 1976. (Consisting of the BJPS article plus additional material from the PhD thesis.)

vol. I *The Methodology of Scientific Research Programmes: Philosophical Papers, Volume 1*, J. Worrall and G. Currie (eds), Cambridge: Cambridge University Press, 1978.

vol. II *Mathematics, Science and Epistemology: Philosophical Papers, Volume 2*, J. Worrall and G. Currie (eds), Cambridge: Cambridge University Press, 1978.

Works by others:

SSR Kuhn, Thomas S., *The Structure of Scientific Revolutions* (2nd edn), Chicago: University of Chicago Press, 1970 (1st edn 1962).

AM Feyerabend, Paul, *Against Method* (3rd edn), London: Verso, 1993 (1st edn 1975).

Chapter 1

Life and character

Imre Lakatos is famous as a philosopher of mathematics and science. As with scientists, it is not normally necessary to know anything about the lives of logicians and methodologists in order to understand their work. So it is with Lakatos. It is possible to understand his philosophy without reference to his biography, and indeed he would have insisted that our evaluation of it should not be affected by biographical or social considerations. For Lakatos, theories should succeed or fail on their logical merits only. However, there is an important question which can only be addressed in the context of his life as a whole: why was Lakatos a rationalist? Rationalism, the view that Reason can and must prevail over Will, was not a conclusion for Lakatos, it was a premise. In order to see why Lakatos took rationalism as his starting point and guiding principle we must look to his early life in Hungary and Russia. There he experienced the efforts of authoritarian governments to impose doctrinaire constraints on the work of scientists and philosophers. As a result, Lakatos was always conscious of the dangers posed to Reason by entrenched dogma in all areas of inquiry, and this concern helped to mould his mature work.

Thus Lakatos' biography can answer questions about his motivations. It can also offer clues regarding his methods. His Marxist education equipped him with a conception of philosophy quite at odds with that normally found in English-speaking academia. For Lakatos, philosophy is not the contemplation of eternal verities but is, rather, an effort to interpret the present in the light of the past with a view to shaping the future. To explain this fact, and others concerning Lakatos' choices of questions and techniques, one must take account of the intellectual environment from which he sprang.

Lakatos was born Imre Lipsitz in Debrecen on 9 November 1922. His father was a strict observer of the Jewish Sabbath, and from 1932 Lakatos attended a Jewish *Realgymnasium* (a secondary school with an emphasis on the sciences).

The Nazis did not begin their occupation of Hungary until March 1944. However, there had always been close economic and cultural ties with Germany, and these links were used by the Nazis to foster fascist elements within Hungary. Moreover, Hungarians were still smarting from the Treaty of Trianon (1920) which stripped their country of over two thirds of its territory and 60 per cent of its population. Some Hungarians saw an alliance with Hitler as a means to reverse these losses. Hungary had a domestic tradition of anti-semitism, part of which had come to associate Jews with bolshevism, and all of which was content to blame the Jewish population for the political strife and economic hardship of the inter-war period. On the other hand, Hungary also had a tradition of resistance to Habsburg rule. For this section of Hungarian opinion, Hitler's *Reich* was yet another threat to Hungarian independence. The Regent, Miklós Horthy of Nagybánya, was anxious that Hungary should not repeat the mistake of ending a world war on the losing side. To this end, he attempted to cultivate both sets of warring powers simultaneously. From 1938 onwards Hungarian governments appeased Hitler by passing a sequence of laws reducing the number of Jews in the professions, barring them from public office and outlawing marriage between Jews and Christians. These measures were rewarded with the return to Hungary of territory previously ceded to Czechoslovakia and Romania. On the other hand, when war broke out Hungary initially remained neutral and opened its borders to Polish refugees.

The policy of vacillation collapsed early in 1941, and Hungary entered the war on the side of the Axis. The strain on the Hungarian economy of supplying the German war effort led to inflation and some restrictions on the availability of food. These effects fuelled anti-German feeling, as did the widespread conviction that Hungarian troops were being used as cannon-fodder. The tiny Hungarian Communist Party tried to exploit this discontent, but only achieved the execution of its local leaders (many of the most senior Hungarian communists were sheltering in Moscow). From 1940, all Jewish males of military age were conscripted into 'labour companies' which were little more than mobile concentration camps. In addition to this and the other anti-Jewish laws, about 25,000 Jews were deported to Poland and Hungarian troops took part in a massacre of Serbs and Jews in the Novi Sad area. When the Nazis eventually occupied Hungary in the spring of 1944, they were able to set about the extermination of Hungarian Jewry in earnest. Over 450,000 people were deported to Poland, with the willing assistance of the Hungarian state police. This figure included non-Jewish opponents of the régime, but it chiefly consisted of Hungary's provincial Jewish population. Widespread anti-German sentiments rarely hardened into armed resistance to the occupation. Thus, in spite of Horthy's efforts, Hungary's identification with the Nazi cause increased just as the tide of war turned against the Axis.

Lakatos used a false identity to escape the labour gangs and the deportations, unlike many of his family and friends, including his mother and grandmother who died in Auschwitz. During the occupation he worked for a Marxist resistance group, living for some time under the assumed name of Tibor Molnár. He adopted the name Lakatos ('Locksmith') early in 1945, after the Russian invasion of Hungary. He seems to have chosen this name with some care, after consultation with a professor of Hungarian literature. At about this time he converted to Calvinism. This, according to his childhood friend Gábor Vajda,[1] was part of an effort to become fully Hungarian, as he saw Calvinism as the 'Hungarian' form of Christianity (the religious divide between Catholics and Calvinists is realised geographically in Hungary, with Debrecen lying in the eastern, Calvinist part of the country). He may also have been influenced in his choice by the replacement (in August 1944) of the Nazi puppet prime minister Döme Sztójay with the moderate General Géza Lakatos (it was Sztójay who introduced the compulsory wearing of yellow stars for Hungarian Jews). This anxiety over questions of identity was not simply a case of the perennial Jewish problem of finding a tolerable position on the continuum between total immersion in Jewish life and complete assimilation to the host culture. Hungarians had to cope with their own history. Not only were they on the losing side in the Second World War, they were on the *wrong* side. Moreover, the question of identity had been tied up with simple personal survival for some time. As the Hungarian historian György Száraz explains:

> [In the 1930s] it was useful to be a full-blooded Turanian Hungarian even with a German grandmother, later it was advisable to appear a pure Aryan with a Jewish great-grandfather; still later the Slovak mason granddad graduated to a German masterbuilder of Szepes County, to prove links with the German race. The face-lifting continued after 1945, before the political screening committees, with changed emphasis. Some relatives – say a 1919 red soldier, an emigrant Octoberist – were quickly brought back into the family, while others were erased. Then it came to pass around 1950 that the great-grandfather of Jewish extraction whom the family took back into grace would have to be made to disappear again, since he was a capitalist, but the German grandmother could be brought back in exchange, as a working peasant woman.[2]

Lakatos' change of name and his dalliance with Calvinism were parts of his answer to a question posed to all Hungarians.

Lakatos studied mathematics, physics and philosophy at the University of Debrecen before the occupation. After the war, he completed his education at the prestigious Eötvös College in Budapest, where he was politically active on the left. In 1947, he was made a secretary in the Ministry of Education with responsibility for the 'democratic reform of higher education' (the Hungarian Communist Party had been very small during the war and there was a shortage of committed Marxists to fill government posts).[3] At this time he was also a research student of the Hegelian-Marxist philosopher György Lukács, and his published work was mostly about literature and politics. Lakatos travelled to Moscow University in 1949.

On his return in the spring of 1950 he was arrested, charged with 'revisionism' and imprisoned for almost four years (including one year in solitary confinement). The exact reason for his arrest is unclear. Lakatos' political zealotry and abrasive manner made him enemies within the Party. Higher education was in turmoil owing to a rapid increase in student numbers combined with extensive political interference. Efforts to force ideological conformity in scientific and artistic life presented intellectuals with a choice between defiance (which led to prison or the labour camps) and feigned obedience. Thinkers developed the art of writing in such a way that their peers would understand their real message while the censor would see only Stalinist orthodoxy. From the summer of 1949 onwards, a stream of Party members were tried for 'left-wing deviance' or right-wing 'revisionism'. Long-standing communists were accused of Nazi collaboration; those who had fought fascism in Spain were denounced as 'cosmopolitan traitors'; Jews were typically branded 'hirelings of Zionism'. By the time Stalin's death (in 1953) brought the worst of the purges to an end, several thousand Party members had been imprisoned, tortured or executed and many more had been stripped of their Party membership.

On his release Lakatos returned to academia. Between 1954 and 1956 Lakatos worked on probability and measure-theory under the mathematician Alfred Rényi. Crucially, one of his tasks was to translate György Pólya's *How to Solve It* into Hungarian (Pólya, working in America, wrote *How to Solve It* for his undergraduates). At the same time, he began to question the entire edifice of Marxist thought. Gábor Vajda reports that in the summer of 1956 Lakatos asked repeatedly 'What is Marxism?' When friends and colleagues offered replies, Lakatos retorted, 'You are speaking about objective knowledge or scientific method. Why do you insist on calling it Marxism?' Other recently-released victims of the purges agitated for justice from the government. Meanwhile, the Hungarian economy (having previously supplied the Habsburg and Nazi empires) had now to serve the Soviet Union. This strain was exacerbated by poor planning. In March 1956, resistance to censorship led to the formation within the Young Communist Organisation of a Budapest student discussion group, the Petőfi Circle, of which Lakatos was a member. Through the summer and autumn the Petőfi Circle staged a sequence of well-attended debates in which the régime was so heavily criticised that two speakers were temporarily expelled from the Party. On 23 October, an anti-Soviet demonstration precipitated a thirteen-day revolution. One week into the revolt Budapest was awash with new newspapers and pamphlets listing the demands and appeals of hastily-formed councils and committees. The 'National Committee of the Hungarian Academy of Sciences' was formed on 30 October and issued a statement the same day. Written by Lakatos and two others, it called on academics and scientists around the world to support the Hungarian uprising, and contained the following paragraph:

> The National Committee of the Hungarian Academy of Sciences takes a stand for the true freedom of science. Scientists are to be guided by no other authority but their own scientific integrity. We demand that every scientific view be allowed free expression in words as in writing, at universities, scientific institutions and before any public forum, free of all restriction by any power, free of all political or moral pressure.
>
> (Archive, 1.10)

One week later the revolution was put down by Soviet troops and a Moscow-approved government was installed. Lakatos left Hungary for Vienna on 25 November 1956.

In 1957 he secured a Rockefeller fellowship to King's College, Cambridge where (supervised by R.B. Braithwaite) he wrote a PhD thesis, a later version of which was eventually published as *Proofs and Refutations*. Pólya (whom Lakatos met in 1958) suggested that he should use the Descartes–Euler conjecture as a case-study. On taking his doctorate in 1960 he joined Popper at the London School of Economics, where he remained until his early death. In 1969 he was appointed Professor of Logic. During this time, his philosophical interests broadened to include physical science, and he developed his 'methodology of scientific research programmes'.

Lakatos' political experiences in Hungary produced in him an unswerving commitment to the principle of academic autonomy expressed in the statement issued during the Hungarian revolution. He saw a threat to that principle in the student unrest of 1968, and rallied to its defence. As he explained in a letter to the Director of the London School of Economics:

> As an undergraduate I witnessed the demands of Nazi students at my University to suppress 'Jewish-liberal-marxist influence' expressed in the syllabuses. . . . Later I was a graduate student at Moscow University when resolutions of the Central Committee of the Communist Party determined syllabuses in genetics and sent the dissenters to death. I also remember when students demanded that Einstein's 'bourgeois relativism' (i.e. his relativity theory) should not be taught.
>
> (vol. II, p. 247)

In short: ideological interference leads to bad science. Science only works if ideas are judged according to their logical merits alone, and it is a necessary (but not sufficient) condition that the scientific community should be free from ideological pressure. Lakatos built this thought into his technical philosophy of science, and it motivated him in his battles with less rationalistically-inclined colleagues.

Later in the same letter he predicted the consequences of allowing militant students onto the University Senate:

> The most sensitive agenda will be discussed and agreed upon in a Director's informal caucus before the Senate meeting and driven though without discussion to avoid Maoist filibuster. They will be sprung on the Senate under 'any other business' in order to avoid previous build up of student pressure.
>
> (vol. II, p. 252)

Lakatos appreciated that freedom may be undermined even by the well-intentioned efforts of its defenders. Reason may be endangered as much by bad thinking as by bad people. In Lakatos' view, the only effective way to defend freedom is to make clear distinctions, between logic and psychology; between science and pseudo-science; and in this case, between the 'constructive' student demand for the right to criticise the university and the 'destructive' demand to take part in its decision-making processes.

His insistence on sharp distinctions led Lakatos, in his own words, to 'think of history as an apocalyptic struggle between angels and devils' (Archive, 12.1, item 11). This caused violent disagreements with friends and colleagues, who were occasionally told that their views were so dangerous that they ought to be shot. Lakatos rarely intended these clashes to be taken personally. He saw no contradiction in combining vehement philosophical conflict with warm friendship. He was that paradoxical thing, a passionate rationalist. Lakatos died on 2 February 1974, aged 51.

Chapter 2

Proofs and Refutations

Proofs and Refutations first came to public notice as an article in the *British Journal for the Philosophy of Science*. Based on part of Lakatos' Cambridge PhD thesis *Essays in the Logic of Mathematical Discovery* (which he completed in 1961) it was published in four parts during 1963 and 1964. Long though this essay was, it only dealt with the *informal* history of the Euler conjecture (see below). The objection that modern mathematics is formal and does not suffer the uncertainties and refutations of informal mathematics was therefore left unanswered. Later in his life Lakatos hoped to write a book on the philosophy of mathematics but, distracted by developments in the philosophy of science and troubled in his later years by ill health, he never managed to produce a manuscript. After his death John Worrall and Elie Zahar undertook to gather what material they considered to be suitable into a single volume in lieu of the proposed work. Thus the original *British Journal* essay together with selections from the PhD thesis were published in 1976 as *Proofs and Refutations: the Logic of Mathematical Discovery*. In their introduction the editors express the hope that the extra chapters can meet the objection that Lakatos' work only applies to informal mathematics.

As is usual in such cases, Worrall and Zahar supplemented Lakatos' writings with some editorial commentary of their own. Most of their remarks are simple clarifications, but in some of their footnotes (especially those on pages 56, 125–6, 138 and 146) they indicate what, in their opinion, Lakatos *ought* to have said or what he undoubtedly *would have* said had he lived long enough to feel the force of their arguments.[1] These contributions were no doubt well meant, and since they come from some of Lakatos' closest colleagues and collaborators they cannot be lightly dismissed. However, it is argued below that while they say little that is false, Worrall and Zahar miss the point of Lakatos' argument. This criticism is not new: Davis and Hersh (1982, pp. 353–8) claim that in their editorial notes Worrall and Zahar commit the error of identifying mathematics with its formal shadow. In other words, they fall prey to the very 'formalism' Lakatos set out to oppose. Some of the blame for the mismatch between the text and the editorial commentary must lie with Lakatos himself. There is a discernible change in the tone of Lakatos' writings in English. His thesis refers freely to dialectical philosophy in general and Hegel in particular as respectable resources available to any educated philosopher. As time passed his vocabulary changed and he seemed to embrace the anti-dialectical, anti-Hegelian mood of the Popperian school. The extent to which this change was merely verbal can only be guessed at, but the Worrall-Zahar line requires Lakatos to abandon the central argument of *Proofs and Refutations* altogether. It is part of the argument of this book that, whether he knew it or not, there was always a dialectical-Hegelian element to Lakatos' work.

DIALECTICS

In a letter to Marx Wartofsky[2] written late in his life and long after he came under the influence of Sir Karl Popper, Lakatos expressed a desire to become the founder of a dialectical school in the philosophy of mathematics. What, one might ask, would a dialectical philosophy of mathematics be like? What could it mean to say that Lakatos' philosophy of mathematics was always dialectical?

The word 'dialectics' has had different meanings in different mouths, but for the present purpose dialectical logic may be distinguished from the rest of logic in the following way. Non-dialectical logic (induction as well as deduction) concerns itself with relations of inference between *propositions*, whereas dialectical logic studies the development of *concepts*. Thus, for example, Plato's *Republic* shows a dialectical pattern, for in that work the concept of justice progresses from very simple beginnings to a rich and sophisticated final form. Unfortunately, this distinction is clearer in thought than in practice because concepts, like muscles, are developed by being used. It is by playing a role in arguments for or against propositions in which they appear that concepts advance in sophistication. In the *Republic* Socrates and his circle develop the concept of justice by debating statements in which that concept figures (for example, 'the just man is a happy man'). The pupils in *Proofs and Refutations* debate Euler's formula for polyhedra $V-E+F=2$ (where V=the number of vertices, E=the number of edges and F=the number of faces). In doing so they modify and improve the concept *polyhedron* (among others). Hence, dialectical logic is inextricably tied up with the logic of propositions.

For these reasons, we cannot easily determine whether a piece of argumentation is dialectical or not. However, we may analyse any given argument first from the perspective of non-dialectical logic and then, separately, from the vantage point of dialectics. That is, we may ask, first *is there a valid inference from the premises to the conclusion*? Then we may ask (from the dialectical side) *do the central concepts in this argument advance in sophistication during its course*?

Notice that we cannot simultaneously answer both these questions affirmatively. For, if a concept mutates during the course of the argument then from the perspective of non-dialectical logic the argument commits the fallacy of equivocation. That is to say, it is not permitted in non-dialectical logic to use a term in more than one sense. But in a dialectical development, this is precisely what happens; 'justice' means something different at the end of the *Republic* than it did at the beginning. On the other hand, if the inference from premises to conclusion is valid, then the central concepts must remain fixed from one end of the argument to the other, in which case there is no dialectical development. It is, of course, possible to answer both questions negatively.

Writing in which concepts are constantly in flux can be very hard to read unless some literary device is used to signal the changes as they happen. One such device is the dialogue form. Usually, each character in a philosophical dialogue represents a particular stage in the evolution of the concept in hand, and it is not uncommon for such a character to introduce himself by giving his definition of that concept, so that we know precisely the stage for which he stands. To return to the *Republic*, when Thrasymachus enters the argument his first contribution is to offer a definition of justice (as that which benefits the strong). Lakatos uses a pattern like this in *Proofs and Refutations*, where some of the students in his dialogue introduce themselves by adding modifications to the concept *polyhedron*. Later, the students come to stand for recognisable methodological and philosophical doctrines.

The dialogue form may also be used to defuse the suggestion that the writer is fighting straw men. Philosophical writing is often populated by idealised figures such as 'the relativist' or 'the nihilist'. Readers might sometimes wonder whether the view under attack is one that anyone ever held. Plato has little to fear on this score because the characters in his dialogues are usually based on real people and use their names. The Socrates in the dialogues is a fictional character based on the real man; there was a real teacher of rhetoric called Gorgias; a real youth called Alcibiades; and so on. Of course, Plato's characters are chosen to represent particular philosophical tendencies. It may be that the historical Gorgias did not instantiate the type 'rhetoric teacher' quite as perfectly as Plato's Gorgias, but this sort of discrepancy does not matter, because Plato was writing philosophy, not biography or history. Plato's Gorgias exemplifies a recognisable type, and the use of a real name reminds us that such people really did exist. Lakatos took his pupils' names from the Greek alphabet rather than from the pages of history, but he connects his fictional debate with actual mathematics and philosophy by the use of detailed footnotes. Occasionally he even puts the words of real mathematicians and philosophers into the mouths of his characters. These historical footnotes make it impossible to accuse Lakatos of inventing a thesis just to knock it down or of reading patterns into the history of mathematics which never really happened. Critics must restrict themselves to arguing (as some do) that the patterns of mathematical reasoning in *Proofs and Refutations* are not typical. This kind of dispute can only be resolved by extensive historical research, just as it is an empirical question whether Gorgias really did represent a common type (the teacher of rhetoric) in Plato's Athens.

Thus far, then, our question 'what would a dialectical philosophy of mathematics be like?' may take the following provisional answer. The students in *Proofs and Refutations* make mathematical arguments using the concept *polyhedron*. In so doing, they change that concept for the better. Dialectical philosophy of mathematics studies the process by which mathematical argument improves mathematical concepts.

We should note, however, that the philosophical study of mathematical dialectics cannot be a matter of identifying some uniform recipe for better concepts, because the path from simplicity to sophistication varies subtly according to the subject matter. Rather, the dialectical philosopher of mathematics studies individual historical episodes which he hopes will turn out to be typical of a sufficiently broad range of cases to be interesting. Some critics seem to have been misled into thinking that Lakatos imagined himself to have discovered *the unique* logic of mathematical discovery.[3] In his original thesis, Lakatos denies that any such thing exists. The teacher of the fictional class complains that:

> Nothing bores me more than the hopeless effort to build up a perfect *system* of heuristic rules. One can point out some tentative rules which may help us to avoid some deeply entrenched wrong heuristic habits. But attempting to turn heuristics into a system of rules which claim to take account of the art of discovery seems to me pathological.

(Thesis, p. 75)[4]

With this warning in mind, we may divide the logical patterns in *Proofs and Refutations* into two groups.

First, there are those cases where the concept of a polyhedron is altered by the presentation of a new kind of geometrical object. So, for example, pupil Alpha comes up with the 'hollow cube', that is, a solid cube with a cubic space inside it (P&R, p. 13, fig. 5). If this is a polyhedron, then Euler's conjecture is false, for in this case $V-E+F=4$. Pupil Delta objects that this 'hollow cube' is not a polyhedron, but rather two polyhedral surfaces. The class (or in reality, the mathematical community) has to decide whether the 'hollow cube' should be counted as a polyhedron or not. As a result of this decision, whichever way it goes, the concept *polyhedron* is a little more clearly defined than hitherto. Before the 'hollow cube' turned up no-one knew whether it would count as a polyhedron, and the concept was, in that respect, vague. Thus, the arrival of a new kind of object forces the class to develop the concept *polyhedron* if only by deciding whether or not it applies to the new object.

Second, there are cases where the concept is altered by the presentation of a new proof. The teacher in the dialogue introduces a proof of the Euler conjecture due to Cauchy. In this proof a face is removed from the polyhedron and the remaining network of faces is stretched flat onto a plane. This proof changed the concept profoundly, for it shifted the study of polyhedra from the theory of solids to topology. Cauchy's thought experiment cannot be carried out on a solid. It is only possible if one thinks of a polyhedron as a network of polygons (i.e. as a surface). Moreover, these two kinds of influence, new objects and new proofs, can interconnect. For example, when Alpha presents the 'hollow cube', Delta objects that it cannot be a polyhedron because Cauchy's thought-experiment cannot be carried out on it. The proof is so impressive that it effectively becomes a criterion for the concept *polyhedron*. In other words, Cauchy's proof provides a reason for not admitting the 'hollow cube' into the class of polyhedra. This is only the most simple example of interaction between proofs and counterexamples, and Lakatos' detailed exploration of these relationships culminates in the 'method of proofs and refutations'. This pattern starts with a conjectured theorem and a proof. When a counterexample appears, one examines the proof to find the (possibly implicit) false assumption responsible for the error. This 'guilty lemma' (to use Lakatos' misleading terminology) is then built into the theorem as a condition. If this pattern is repeated sufficiently often, these conditions may accumulate to the point where they collectively define a new concept.

These patterns of conceptual growth through the interaction of proofs and refutations are complicated still further when one considers that concepts do not exist in isolation. Changes to the meaning of 'polyhedron' induce modifications of related terms such as 'edge' or 'vertex'. For example, the shift from the theory of solids to topology caused by Cauchy's proof changes the meaning of 'face' in such a way that it becomes intelligible to speak of faces that intersect each other. This is the point of the 'urchin' (or small stellated dodecahedron) introduced by Gamma (P&R, p. 16, fig. 7). In this sense, each modification of the meaning of (in this case) 'polyhedron' brings a new theoretical language into being. Every time this happens, the problem at hand must be translated into the new language. The translation may be explicit (as in the case of Epsilon's proof of Euler's conjecture, which requires that the geometrical problem be translated into the language of vector algebra). However, in the rest of *Proofs and Refutations* the linguistic shifts are unnoticed until pointed out by Pi (who does most of the talking in the section on concept-formation).

Thus, what starts out as a mathematical investigation into Euler's formula becomes a study of the art of mathematical discovery, which in turn becomes an examination of the growth of mathematical concepts. In other words, *Proofs and Refutations* turns out to be an essay on dialectics in the sense described above. That is, it illustrates some of the ways in which mathematicians can improve concepts even as those concepts are put to use in arguments. It is also an example of dialectical reasoning itself, for some of its central concepts mutate as the debate progresses. At the outset, the word 'heuristics' means hints and tips for finding plausible conjectures and proof-ideas. Lakatos learned about heuristics in this sense from the work of George Pólya. For example, Pólya notes that theorems in plane geometry often have three-dimensional counterparts. Hence, if we want to discover new theorems in three-dimensional geometry, we might do well to try working up from plane theorems. This sense of heuristics as *ars inveniendi* is a little different from its ordinary English sense. In English, a heuristic is a psychological device to help the finite human mind to understand something difficult. Pólya's heuristic exploits objective features of mathematics, rather than subjective quirks of human psychology. It is in that sense rational, though fallible. By the end of *Proofs and Refutations*, 'heuristics' has come to mean the study of conceptual growth through argument, or in other words, dialectics.

The development of the concept of heuristic illustrates another feature of dialectical argument. To be persuasive, one should start with a version of the concept in hand that is recognisable and unobjectionable to one's intended audience. The definitions of justice offered to Socrates in the opening pages of the *Republic* were intended to reflect the commonsense of Plato's Athens. In *Proofs and Refutations* the concept of heuristic starts its dialectical journey from Pólya's plausible reasoning because these simple techniques are recognisable to anyone with any experience of mathematics. If the dialectical argument is sufficiently compelling, the reader will follow the development through to the rich, sophisticated end-point. Plato hopes to show us the advantages of his preferred conception of justice over common understanding of the term from which he started. In

Lakatos' case, the claim is that if we start out with Pólya-style heuristics, we must eventually end up with dialectics.

As Lakatos develops the meaning of 'heuristic', he also pursues a dialectic on 'counterexample'. At the outset, a counterexample is just a case which demonstrates the falsehood of a general conjecture. As the dialogue unfolds the class discovers that strange polyhedra can affect their investigation in more subtle ways than simply by refuting their hypothesis. There may be cases which, while they pose no logical threat to the theorem, expose shortcomings in the attendant proof. For example, there is a proof of the Euler formula due to Legendre which only works for convex or near-convex polyhedra (P&R, p. 60). The great stellated dodecahedron (P&R, p. 61, fig. 15) is not convex (or near-convex), but nevertheless the Euler formula is true of it. Faced with this example, the class searches for a more general proof. Meeting little success, the pupils are persuaded to consider cases for which $V-E+F$ does not equal two *and* which fall outside the scope of their best proof. These cases offer no logical problems for the theorem (since it is not meant to apply to them) nor do they suggest that the proof is insufficiently comprehensive (as the great stellated dodecahedron did). However, they do suggest that the investigation has been unnecessarily restricted to cases for which $V-E+F=2$. The class discovers that it is possible to account for the 'Euler characteristic' ($V-E+F$) of a great many polyhedra aside from those for which it equals two.

The lesson is that an investigation can be driven forward by cases which present no strictly logical difficulties for the theorem in hand, but which expose some lack of generality in either the theorem or its associated proof. Lakatos called these cases 'heuristic counterexamples', to distinguish them from 'logical' counterexamples (which really are inconsistent with the theorem in question). Thus, within the text, the term 'counterexample' has come to cover any case which presents a criticism of an existing theorem or proof. Moreover, the concept has developed some internal structure since there are now two sorts of counterexample: logical ones and heuristic ones.

Having established this distinction between logical and heuristic counterexamples, Lakatos (using the voice of Pi) connects it with his thesis that every new object (or new proof, for that matter) induces a further determination in the theoretical language. In the early part of the dialogue, the development of the relevant mathematical concepts went unnoticed by the pupils. Pi argues that at the outset, 'polyhedron' meant the Platonic solids and similarly well-behaved objects. The class unconsciously expanded the concept to include solids with cavities, tunnels and ring-shaped faces as these objects were discovered. The point is that given the original meaning of 'polyhedron', none of these exotica was a logical counterexample to the claim that *for all polyhedra, V-E+F=2*. They only came to be logical counterexamples once the mathematical vocabulary had been amended so that they counted as polyhedra. As Pi puts it:

> Usually, when a 'counterexample' is presented, you have a choice: either you refuse to bother with it, since it is not a counterexample at all in your *given* language L_1, or you agree to change your language by concept-stretching and accept the counterexample in your new language L_2.

> (P&R, p. 93)

In other words, what seemed to be logical counterexamples were at first nothing of the sort. They were, in fact, heuristic counterexamples. It was only when the language shifted under pressure from 'heuristic' criticism that they became logical counterexamples. As such they could then be used to force a revision of the theorem. Thus, heuristic counterexamples turn out to be just those cases which bring about a change in mathematical meanings. Dialectic (or heuristic as Lakatos calls it here) is the argumentative process by which the mathematical community persuades itself to stretch or replace part of its theoretical vocabulary.

Lakatos was convinced that these linguistic changes can have a rational basis, that there can be objective grounds for developing a concept this way or that. He also thought that the study of such reasoned language-shifts had been neglected as a result of philosophical prejudice. He has Pi remark that given the dilemma outlined above, 'According to traditional static rationality you would have to make the first choice. Science teaches you to make the second' (P&R, p. 93). 'Static rationality' for Lakatos is any philosophical view which refuses to treat the development of concepts as a rational process and which insists that meanings remain fixed from one end of an argument to the other. The nineteenth-century union of formal logic and mathematics produced a family of such views. As a result, thought Lakatos, 'traditional static rationality' came to dominate the philosophy of mathematics.

FORMALISM

Mathematics and logic were strangers until the second half of the nineteenth century. Syllogistic logic seemed to offer neither insight into mathematical reasoning nor any interesting problems for mathematicians to work on. The nineteenth century rapprochement was caused by changes in logical practice as mathematicians revised their conception of proof, and by developments in logical theory.

On the theory side, logic became a branch of mathematics as the formal systems of Frege, Boole and others replaced the syllogistic logics of their predecessors. Not only did the new mathematical logic offer interesting problems for mathematicians, but it promised insights into mathematical and scientific forms of argument. For example, Frege's logic seemed to offer a precise analysis of mathematical induction. However, in order to bring mathematical logic to bear on mathematics itself, it was necessary to identify mathematics with its axiomatic abstraction. That is to say, it was necessary to treat mathematical theories as if they were axiomatised formal systems with explicit rules of inference. Lakatos referred to this view in which 'mathematical theories are replaced by formal systems, proofs by certain sequences of well-defined formulae, definitions by "abbreviatory devices" which are "theoretically dispensable" but "typographically convenient" ' (P&R, p. 1) as 'formalism'. This 'formalism' is older and broader than Hilbert's school of philosophy. Logicists are usually formalists in Lakatos' sense (I shall adopt his usage), and Lakatos cited Carnap, Church, Peano, Russell and Whitehead as examples (P&R, p. 1, n. 1).

The identification of mathematics with formal abstractions invites us to replace the philosophy of mathematics with mathematical logic. Formalism is therefore pernicious for Lakatos because it leads to the philosophical neglect of everything about mathematics not captured by the formalist abstraction. In particular, formalism sidelines Pólya's work on mathematical heuristic. Indeed, Pólya-style 'plausible reasoning' is not even part of mathematics, for formalism. Most of the history of mathematics resembles Pólya's informal investigations more than it does the formalist axiomatic vision. It follows that 'real' (i.e. formal) mathematics did not begin until the middle of the nineteenth century. Even now, very little of what goes on in mathematics classes counts as mathematics by formalist standards. It is consistent with the spirit of Lakatos' project to add that 'formalism' so defined makes a mystery of the evaluative language of mathematicians. Formalists do not have the theoretical wherewithal to explain why some results are held to be deep and why some proofs are selected for celebration. Formalists cannot explain the difference between a theorem and a corollary, except to say that the theorem occurs in the proof of the corollary, but not *vice versa*. Such an account cannot articulate the difference between the lemma/theorem relationship and the theorem/corollary relationship. None of this means that Lakatos was hostile to mathematical logic itself, which he taught at the London School of Economics.

The formalist domination of the philosophy of mathematics, according to Lakatos, also reflected a change in mathematical practice. On his account, eighteenth-century mathematicians thought of proofs as thought-experiments. On this view, the rigour of a proof lies in the clarity and distinctness of the relevant ideas (in a more or less Cartesian sense). In the following century, mathematicians learned the art of proof-analysis. They had little choice, because a series of strange objects and counter-intuitive results threatened apparently well-established theorems. It was this development in particular that Lakatos hoped to model in the opening part of *Proofs and Refutations*. Now, in order to spot 'guilty lemmas' it is necessary to think of a proof as mathematical logicians currently do, as a sequence of sentences, each derived from its predecessors by the correct application of a valid rule of inference. Moreover, the method of lemma-incorporation tends to load the burden of argument onto the purely logical terms, and the mathematical content of the theorem has less and less to do with its proof (see *Proofs and Refutations*, Chapter 1, §9, 'How Criticism may turn Mathematical Truth into Logical Truth'). With this change in mathematical practice in view, it seemed that mathematics, when perfected, really is a collection of formal systems. In other words, formalism is one of those cases in which a particular historical development (the increasing formalisation of mathematics in the late nineteenth century) is seized upon and given the status of a timeless philosophical thesis.

Lakatos' chief objection to formalism is that it establishes 'static rationality' as the only sort there is. Mathematical logic models those deductive relationships between propositions which obtain in virtue of the propositions' logical forms. The meanings of non-logical symbols play no role in arguments of this sort. Nevertheless those meanings (whatever they may be) must remain fixed from one end of the argument to the other. That is, the logical force of a formal argument depends entirely on the meanings of the logical symbols. However, when the system is interpreted (i.e. the non-logical symbols of the system are given meanings) it is proper to insist that a given symbol takes the same meaning wherever it occurs. Lakatos' charge is not against formal logic itself, for formal arguments exist and merit study. Rather, he complains that the enormous success of mathematical logic led to the neglect of other kinds of logical inquiry. In particular, the study of the development of concepts and the growth of knowledge was marginalised. Indeed, many philosophers (including Popper) elevated this neglect into a principled distinction between the *context of discovery* and *the context of justification*. The context of discovery is the psychological process by which a mathematician or scientist hits upon a conjecture. It might be a matter of spotting a pattern in a lot of collected data, or it might be the result of a dream. The context of justification is the argument by which conjecture is proved. These terms are not very happy, for various reasons. 'Context' suggests the background to something else (but what?) and it is not clear that a context can also be a process. Moreover, 'discovery' is a success-word. A conjecture is only a discovery if it turns out to be true. Popper had an extra difficulty since in his epistemology a proposition cannot be verified (although later versions of his view allow propositions to be 'corroborated').

Terminology aside, the distinction separates the production of conjectures from their evaluation. On this view the *production* of conjectures is philosophically irrelevant and its study should be left to psychologists and sociologists. The *evaluation* of conjectures, on the other hand, is (or at least, should be) a rational process and is therefore the proper concern of epistemology and logic.

Lakatos knew from the work of Pólya that the production of

mathematical conjectures can be a rational undertaking. Pólya's methods for finding likely theorem-candidates and proof-ideas are not infallible (nor did he pretend otherwise). For all that these techniques are fallible, they do represent a kind of rationality. They are, in Pólya's phrase, 'plausible reasoning'. Consequently, it will not do to abandon the study of mathematical discovery to psychologists and sociologists. Many of Pólya's suggestions are specific to particular parts of mathematics, but this is only paradoxical if we insist that logic should be entirely topic-neutral. Of course, it is possible that a mathematician could hit on a true theorem by some occult psychological process that defies logical analysis. Nevertheless, the processes of production and evaluation usually interpenetrate. Even when a conjecture seems to have come from a flash of genius, it is unlikely to be sheer good luck. Even the greatest leaps of insight need some logical scene-setting.

Lakatos did not only deny that the 'context of discovery' must be closed to logical analysis. He challenged the distinction itself. Proofs, for Lakatos, do not just establish the truth of theorems. They can also be engines of discovery. On the other hand, the fruitfulness of a mathematical idea as source of conjectures can also serve as evidence for its truth. In *Proofs and Refutations* Lakatos does not argue directly against the distinction between the contexts of discovery and justification. Instead, he presents a picture of mathematics in which proofs, tests and thought-experiments are so intimately related that it is impossible to say where one context finishes and another starts. He then argues that his account of mathematics is better than that of any formalist, because formalists can only cope with a tiny part of mathematical rationality. The formalist can only account for the proof that a theorem may receive when it is expressed in an axiomatic system using a formal logical language. Lakatos' conception of mathematical rationality includes this proof but also investigates the long informal process by which a problem is readied for translation into a formal system. Hence, his case against the distinction between the contexts of discovery and justification is that his depiction of mathematical reasoning is more comprehensive (and hence better) than those which make use of the distinction.

Lakatos *has* to show that this distinction is misguided because otherwise he leaves the formalist in possession of an argument.

Another way of putting the principle motivating the distinction is to say that epistemology is only concerned with the end products of inquiry. The only question for philosophers is whether these end results are justified (or corroborated, in Popper's case). In modern mathematics, the end product is usually a highly formalised theory. Thus the formalist can appeal to the discovery/justification distinction to argue that even if most mathematical activity does not concern itself with formal abstractions, it is only the end products of this activity that concern the philosopher, and nowadays these end products are highly formalised theories. Hence, formalism in Lakatos' sense of the word entails no philosophical loss. If this argument goes through then dialectical philosophy of mathematics is impossible, for the aim of dialectical analysis is to study the process of mathematical development itself, and not just the output of that process. Notice that in rejecting the distinction between these 'contexts' Lakatos makes no concession to psychologism. As a dialectician, he hopes to examine the growth of mathematics *philosophically*. That is, he hopes to depict it as a rational, objective process (that is why we speak of dialectical logic, not dialectical psychology).

Formalist philosophy of mathematics and the distinction between discovery and justification are both elements of logical positivism. Lakatos' objections to these doctrines are part of a general critique of the logical positivist enterprise:

> According to the logical positivists, the *exclusive* task of philosophy is to construct 'formalised' languages in which artificially congealed states of science are expressed. . . . But such investigations scarcely get underway before the rapid growth of science discards the old 'language system'. Science teaches us not to respect any given conceptual-linguistic framework lest it turn into a conceptual prison, language analysts have a vested interest in at least slowing down this process, in order to justify their linguistic therapeutics.
>
> (P&R, p. 93, n. 1)

In their efforts to avoid psychologism, the logical positivists had decreed that only the finished products of science are suitable for philosophical study. The practical consequence of this was that contemporary science was treated as if it were the final resting place of inquiry, and static, formal logic treated as if it were the only rationality there is. (Note that on most logical positivist views of the matter, an inductive reasoning pattern is formal in the sense that the persuasiveness of the argument lies solely in its form: 'every F so far has been G, so the next F will probably be G' – it makes no difference what 'F' and 'G' mean. Therefore, the point applies equally well to logical positivist philosophy of science as to mathematics.)[5]

Proofs and Refutations is also anti-positivist in its historiography. Logical positivist philosophers of history take the view that to explain an historical event is to subsume it under some general law. Historical knowledge, then, consists of two parts: knowledge of individual historical facts, and knowledge of general historical laws. Historical facts may be individuated and grasped one by one, but a fact is only explicable in so far as it instantiates some law or laws. In other words, positivist philosophers of history offer the same logical analysis in the case of historical knowledge as they do for natural science.[6] What they deny is that an historical episode can be understood and explained in a way that exploits its uniqueness. In *Proofs and Refutations* Lakatos makes no attempt to discover general laws of mathematical development, and in his PhD thesis he explicitly rejected any attempt to search for such laws (see the teacher's remark cited above). Of course, Lakatos holds that logical patterns similar to those in *Proofs and Refutations* are widespread in mathematics, but such similarities do not play the explanatory role assigned to general laws by positivist philosophers of history. When a number of different episodes in the history of mathematics have each been understood and explained as unique historical events, we may be in a position to observe that some likeness obtains between them. Lakatos does not suppose that any such likeness might have a part in explaining why these various events turned out the way they did. He must think, however, that the case he examines is in some sense typical if it is to have any philosophical significance (just as we would be far less interested in Plato's *Gorgias* if we thought that there are no rhetoricians now or in the past apart from Gorgias himself).

It has been suggested[7] that Lakatos' attack on formalism is a little like Hegel's criticism of Kant's moral theory. Hegel argues that Kant offers no more than a formal framework. This Kantian framework (according to Hegel) cannot supply its own content, that is, ethics cannot be generated from logic alone. Similarly,

Lakatos objects that mathematics cannot be understood philosophically if it is replaced by its formal shadow. There may be something in this analogy: certainly some leading formalists (such as Frege and Hilbert) cited Kant as an inspiration. Perhaps we should not be surprised if the most celebrated critic of formalism in the philosophy of mathematics owes a debt to the theorist who identified and criticised the formalism of Kantian philosophy as a whole.

HEGEL

Lakatos' use of the dialogue form may invite a comparison with Plato, and indeed *Proofs and Refutations* shows flashes of wit and irony similar to those in the Socratic dialogues. However, Lakatos claimed inspiration from a different dialectician: 'The three major, apparently incompatible, 'ideological' sources of [the] thesis [that became *Proofs and Refutations*] are Pólya's mathematical heuristic, Hegel's dialectic and Popper's critical philosophy'.[8] Hegel's writing is far more austere than that of Plato or Lakatos. In a dialogue, the dialectical development of concepts is leavened by human drama between the characters. Hegel thought that the use of human mouthpieces for philosophical ideas introduces irrelevant questions which can only distract attention from the logical development of the ideas themselves. Nevertheless, there is a sense in which *Proofs and Refutations* is closer to Hegel than to Plato. Platonic dialogues are typically dominated by Socrates, who talks more than anyone else and directs the conversation towards the truth as he sees it by a combination of logical analysis, tendentious description and verbal bullying. By contrast, the teacher in *Proofs and Refutations* seems to have more faith in the power (or the cunning) of reason than Plato's Socrates. Rather than actively directing the discussion, the teacher is for the most part content to set the initial problem, and to make occasional clarifying remarks. Sometimes he intervenes to prevent the debate from getting locked into a stalemate (as for example on p. 95 when he cuts short an unpromising standoff between Pi and Alpha). There are a few passages where he takes an active part. Most of the time, however, he allows the pupils to work out the arguments for themselves. In this he reflects the Hegelian view that the proper philosophical method is not to pick a thesis and defend it with whatever rhetorical force one can muster, but rather to immerse oneself in the subject matter and thus to allow oneself to become a vehicle for its internal logic.

Hegelian dialectic is often supposed to be a three-step formula: thesis, antithesis, synthesis. It is a matter of some debate whether this picture of Hegel's method is accurate. Certainly, the table of contents of his *Logic* consists almost entirely of triples of sub-sections within triples of sections. At any rate, Lakatos clearly held that philosophy sometimes advances in this manner. In a published conversation with R.H. Popkin, he claims that:

> [The] success [of scientific heuristic] may also yield a new appraisal of the sceptico-dogmatist controversy: it would remove it from the central position it still occupies in the mind of those who have not recognized the basic unity of the opposites and the possibility of their dialectical *'Aufheben'*.[9]

The thought here is that dogmatism and scepticism are two aspects of the same mistake – they both stem from justificationist epistemology. Consequently, neither can defeat the other, and a standoff ensues. Philosophy can only move beyond such a stalemate by unearthing the common error which unites dogmatism and scepticism into a dialectical pair. This view of philosophical progress is thoroughly Hegelian-Marxist.

The *Proofs and Refutations* dialogue sometimes follows the *Aufheben* pattern. For example, in an early part of the discussion (P&R, pp. 15–16, 19–21) pupils Alpha and Delta disagree over whether strange objects such as the twin tetrahedra are polyhedra. Delta refuses to accept such objects as polyhedra, and produces increasingly complex 'monster-barring' definitions in order to exclude them. Alpha accuses him of artificially contracting the sense of 'polyhedron'. This disagreement is not resolved either way, because Delta and Alpha share a mistake. They implicitly agree that there is an objective essence (a Platonic form, perhaps) to which the word 'polyhedron' refers, and a fact of the matter as to whether (e.g.) the twin tetrahedra are instances of this essential form. This shared error is exposed and overcome as the polyhedron-concept is replaced by proof-generated concepts in topology and, eventually, algebra. 'Polyhedron', it turns out, does not denote an objective mathematical category:

As far as naive classification is concerned, nominalists are close to the truth when claiming that the only thing that polyhedra have in common is their name. But after a few centuries of proofs and refutations, as the theory of polyhedra develops, and theoretical classification replaces naive classification, the balance changes in favour of the realist.

(P&R, p. 92, n. 1)

For Lakatos, progress in mathematics means that the concepts employed by mathematicians approximate more and more closely the objective structure of mathematical reality.

Lakatos once described the method of proofs and refutations in terms of the Hegelian triad (P&R, pp. 144-5). In this account, the original conjecture and proof together constitute the thesis. The counterexample is the antithesis. The synthesis is the improved theorem and proof complex which is arrived at by proof-analysis and lemma-incorporation. An important feature of this pattern is that the process of proof and criticism is creative (*pace* Popper), giving rise to new conjectures and new proof-generated concepts. This is possible because the counterexample does not only show that the naive conjecture is false: it points to a specific problem, the solution of which leads to a new conjecture. In Hegelian jargon, the counterexample does not stand in 'bare opposition' to the original conjecture and proof complex but rather offers a 'determinate (i.e. specific) negation' of it. The synthesis in *this* dialectical three-step does not unite the best of the thesis and the antithesis. Rather, the synthesis solves the problem posed by the antithesis for the thesis.

This Hegelian gloss on the method of proofs and refutations occurs in Lakatos' discussion of Seidel's discovery of uniform convergence. He claims that 'The Hegelian language, which I use here, would, I think, generally be capable of describing the various developments in mathematics. (It has, however, its dangers as well as its attractions.)' (P&R, p. 145). The particular danger that Lakatos seems to have had in mind originates in the fact that reason in general, and mathematical dialectic in particular, must be realised in human beings, human institutions and (nowadays) human-built machines. Mathematicians and mathematical institutions are vulnerable to all the ills that flesh is heir to, and consequently there is no guarantee that mathematics will always develop rationally, or indeed at all. The austerity of Hegel's dialectical writing obscures this fact, leaving the impression that logical necessity alone is sufficient to ensure the progress of whatever body of thought is in question. In a footnote, Lakatos briefly turns his attention from Hegel to Marx:

> My concept of the mathematician as the imperfect personification of Mathematics is closely analogous to Marx's concept of the capitalist as the personification of Capital. Unfortunately Marx did not qualify his conception by stressing the imperfect nature of this personification, and that there is nothing inexorable about the realisation of this process. On the contrary, human activity can always suppress or distort the autonomy of alienated processes and can give rise to new ones.
>
> (P&R, p. 146, n. 1)

As we shall see, there is more to Lakatos' fallibilism than the thought that mathematicians can be less than perfect vessels for mathematics. Rather, logic itself underdetermines the future path of mathematics.

Lakatos' mathematical 'Hegelianism' would be of little interest if it consisted only in his having once employed the three-step model of knowledge-growth.[10] It is a familiar fact that this pattern can be 'found' in almost any intellectual field if it is searched for with sufficient ingenuity. To appreciate fully the extent of Lakatos' debt to Hegel, we need to examine his distinction between the 'deductivist' and 'heuristic' mathematical styles.

Lakatos spelled out this distinction in what appears as the second appendix to *Proofs and Refutations*, entitled 'The Heuristic Approach' (drawn from Chapter 3 of his thesis). The prevailing 'Euclidean' (or 'deductivist') methodology, according to Lakatos, requires mathematical work to be presented in a very particular manner:

> This style starts with a painstakingly stated list of *axioms, lemmas* and/or *definitions*. The axioms and definitions frequently look artificial and mystifyingly complicated. One is never told how these complications arose. The list of axioms and definitions is followed by the carefully worded *theorems*. These are loaded with heavy-going conditions; it seems unlikely that anyone should ever have guessed them. The theorem is followed by the *proof*.
>
> (P&R, p. 142)

This 'deductivist' style is pernicious, according to Lakatos, because it hides the struggle through which the finely tuned theorem and its proof-generated definitions were achieved. The original naive conjecture and the critical process of its refinement are banished to history (which conveniently doubles as the 'context of discovery'). Meanwhile, the end product is regarded as an infallible truth, hedged about as it is with proof-generated monster-barring definitions.[11]

Lakatos claims that the 'deductivist' style permits a kind of degeneration, because it allows authors to 'atomise' mathematics, that is, to present proof-generated definitions separately and ahead of the proofs from which they were born. This tearing apart of heuristic connections obscures the 'problem situation' from which the theorem and proof emerged. The 'deductivist' style permits this because its authoritarianism relieves authors of the responsibility of motivating their work. In 'Euclidean' methodology a theorem need not have a point; all it needs is a proof. Lakatos clearly suspected that some contemporary mathematics is indeed pointless:

> Stating the primitive conjecture, showing the proof, the counterexamples, and following the heuristic order up to the theorem and to the proof-generated definition would dispel the authoritarian mysticism of abstract mathematics, and would act as a brake on degeneration. A couple of case-studies in this degeneration would do much good for mathematics. Unfortunately the deductivist style and the atomization of mathematical knowledge protect 'degenerate' papers to a very considerable degree.
>
> (P&R, p. 154; see also P&R, p. 98, n. 2)

In Lakatos' alternative style of mathematics, the 'heuristic approach', a 'distilled' history of the theorem and its proof is the chief part of the exposition. This compressed and streamlined history starts not with definitions but with a problem or a question. A naive answer ('primitive conjecture') is offered, and criticised. Through criticism the solution is improved and eventually the final result emerges. Thus the result is motivated by the initial question and its technicalities are explained by the narrative of conjectures and criticism.

To see what this has to do with Hegel, we must improve our account of Hegelian dialectics beyond the crude thesis-antithesis-synthesis formula. Hegel attempted to characterise dialectical logic by contrasting it with mathematics:

> [Mathematical] proof . . . follows a path that begins somewhere or other without indicating as yet what relation such a beginning will have to the result that will emerge. In its progress it takes up *these* particular determinations and relations, and lets others alone, without its being immediately clear what the controlling necessity is; an external purpose governs this procedure.
>
> (Hegel 1977, §44, p. 25)

In fact, what Hegel describes here is mathematics *in the deductivist style* (indeed, it is clear from the surrounding text that Hegel has Euclid in mind). Deductivist presentations of theorems and their proofs begin with definitions and axioms 'without indicating as yet what relation such a beginning will have to the result that will emerge'. The 'controlling necessity' is the heuristic background to the proof. That is what explains the choice of 'determinations' (definitions, axioms and lemmas). This 'purpose' is only 'external' because Euclidean methodology requires that the heuristic background be banished from the scene. In other words, Hegel's distinction between dialectical and so-called 'mathematical' reasoning is a direct ancestor of Lakatos' distinction between the heuristic and deductive styles. Hegel's claim is that in dialectical reasoning, each stage grows out of and is explained by what came before. There is no need to take definitions on trust, in the hope that they will turn out to be just right for the job. Lakatos' claim is that mathematics done in the heuristic style has the same virtue.

Hence, Lakatos' use of Hegelian jargon was not casual. Hegel's dialectical logic is an attempt to represent the emergence of new concepts as a rational process, which is exactly what Lakatos wanted to achieve for mathematics. Hegel's method was to write a special kind of 'distilled' or 'philosophically comprehended' history ('distilled' is Lakatos' word; 'philosophically comprehended' is the Hegelian expression). Lakatos chose to cast his essay in this idiom because he was working on a mathematical version of the same problem.

In spite of the presence of these Hegelian elements in *Proofs and Refutations*, it should not be imagined that Lakatos was a slavish follower of Hegel. To begin with, Lakatos sided with

Popper against Hegel on the question of 'historicism'. Historicism (as defined by Popper) is the thesis that there can be a predictive science of human activity. As his criticism of Marx shows, Lakatos did not think that human inquiry must necessarily terminate in absolute knowledge (or indeed in knowledge of any sort), nor did he think that human history must end in a triumph for freedom and reason. Even if the development of mathematics were unhindered by inconvenient wars and frailties of the flesh, there is no reason to suppose that there must always be a unique path forwards:

SIGMA So the 'theory of solids', the original 'naive' realm of the Euler conjecture, dissolves, and the remodelled conjecture reappears in projective geometry if proved by Gergonne, in analytical topology if proved by Cauchy, in algebraic topology if proved by Poincaré.

(P&R, p. 90)

Even if we had a guarantee that mathematics will always progress (which we do not), there would still be no knowing what direction this progress would take.

Moreover, Lakatos had no truck with Hegelian 'speculative proofs' of scientific theories. In these 'proofs' Hegel tried to show that the scientific orthodoxies of his day were necessarily true, by deriving the empirical theories from the fundamental categories of his metaphysical system. Lakatos did not criticise these 'proofs' directly, but we can make an educated guess at what he might have said. These 'speculative proofs' present the same danger as the perfectly clear scientific languages dreamt of by positivists and the immutable language-games of the later Wittgenstein: 'science teaches us not to respect any given conceptual-linguistic framework lest it should turn into a conceptual prison' (P&R, p. 93, n. 1). The point stands even if the framework in question has the majestic allure of Hegel's system. If this guess is correct, then (together with his anti-historicism) it suggests that Lakatos parted company with Hegel at just the point where Hegel turns against fallibilism.

FALLIBILISM

Proofs and Refutations is often read as an attempt to apply Popper's philosophy of science to mathematics. This reading is not wholly false, because Lakatos did hold that mathematics advances through criticism and refutations (and indeed, Lakatos did cite Popper as one of his 'ideological' sources). However, Popper was contemptuous of dialectic, and this led to a number of important differences with Lakatos. As we have seen, Lakatos thought that the production of conjectures can be a rational activity and can therefore be studied philosophically. In particular, he thought that criticism can be productive of new conjectures (since a counterexample does not merely show *that* a conjecture is false, but may indicate *why* it is false and *how* it can be fixed). Furthermore, Lakatos thought that the refutation of an established mathematical theory is a far more complex logical event than Popper's model. The role of criticism is not simply to confront the theory with recalcitrant phenomena. Rather it is to force a shift to a new conceptual framework, in search of deeper theorems and proofs. What Lakatos did have in common with Popper was *fallibilism*. This is the view that any of our accepted theories might turn out to be false. In other words, nothing is certain.

Fallibilism in mathematics is open to two objections. First, it may be objected, mathematicians can give logically perfect proofs. If a proof is cast in a formal language with explicit rules of inference there can be no logical gaps, so how can there be any doubts about the conclusion? Second, it may be claimed that there can be no serious doubts about simple equations like 1+2=3. These (runs the objection) are surely self-evident. If Lakatos were simply a mathematical Popperian, then these objections might be decisive. They are not, because Lakatos' fallibilism follows from his insistence that non-trivial refutations always involve conceptual development.

Lakatos addresses the first objection in the second chapter of *Proofs and Refutations*. Here the pupil Epsilon defends a fully formalised proof (which is in fact due to Poincaré) of a version of the Euler conjecture. Before he can do so, he needs to translate the problem into a suitably formal language. First, he replaces the particular concepts *vertex*, *edge*, *face* and *polyhedron* with the general concept of a *k–polytope*. An edge, for example, is a 1–polytope. Polyhedra (3–polytopes) are characterised by *incidence matrices*, which are tables recording which vertices belong to which edges and which edges to which faces. The effect is to translate the problem into logical, set-theoretical and arithmetical terms, and to remove all mechanical and geometrical references. In this 'pure' idiom he defines 'bound', 'boundary' and 'closed' (and a few new terms, such as 'k–chain' and 'circuit'). With this terminology he can state his theorem: *All polyhedra, all of whose circuits bound, are Eulerian* (P&R, p. 114). Next, he reformulates the theorem in a way which shows that 'it is a theorem about the number of dimensions of certain vector spaces determined by the incidence matrix' (P&R, p. 116). He is then able to prove his theorem by appeal to established results in vector algebra.

The question now is, what has he proved? In his definitions, Epsilon took as an axiom: *all vertices have the empty set*, claiming that this has the same status as *all faces have edges*. Asked whether the cylinder is a counterexample to his theorem, he replies that it is not because in the cylinder 'the empty set does not bound' (P&R, p. 121). The condition of the theorem is that 'all circuits bound'. The empty set, considered as a circuit, does not bound, so the theorem is safe. The remarkable thing is that Epsilon has defined 'bound' and 'circuit' in such a way that we can meaningfully ask whether the empty set bounds, and yet he claims not to have deformed the pre-translation concepts in any way, merely to have revealed their essences. If the class had been asked ahead of Epsilon's translation whether the empty set bounds in this or that polyhedron, they should quite properly have been baffled. Clearly, something has happened to the old geometrical concepts during the translation.

Epsilon's translation-definitions stretch and determine the concepts in hand so as to introduce a new, more explanatory theoretical framework. The point is particularly clear in the case of 'bound'. What is the reason for exhibiting the heptahedron, if not to manipulate the development of the concept of *bounding* in exactly the same way that the exhibition of the picture-frame guided the evolution of *polyhedron*? Epsilon's definitions are acceptable, not because they exhibit the essences of familiar concepts, nor because he is free to stipulate as he wishes, but because they permit him to produce a proof that 'explains both the Eulerian character of ordinary polyhedra and the Eulerian character of star-polyhedra at one blow' (P&R, p. 120). Epsilon's new theoretical framework has to struggle for acceptance in precisely the same way as every other significant innovation in the story. Much of the preamble to the proof consists of Epsilon trying to convince his peers that his definitions are a natural and progressive development of the existing conceptual scheme. The point is, Epsilon/Poincaré's theorem and proof are an advance not because they achieve final certainty, but because they unify diverse phenomena and explain the shortcomings of their predecessors.

Poincaré's proof is defeasible because his theorem is not fully general. It does not have anything to say about 'Lhuilier examples' such as the picture-frame with an Euler characteristic of two. Of course, these cases are not logical counterexamples, but they show the limited explanatory power of the theorem. If there were some sort of revolution in the informal theory of polyhedra that seemed to offer a unified explanation of the properties of all these objects, then Epsilon's concept-stretching definitions might suddenly seem unreasonable. Armed with a new informal theoretical perspective, we might refuse to accept his subtle reworking of the concepts of *bounding* and *polyhedron*. Epsilon's theorem would then have been heuristically falsified, just as Delta's theorem was heuristically falsified by the early 'monsters'. Lakatos makes a version of this point in a footnote:

> Adequacy criteria [for translations] may change with the emergence of new problems which may occasion a change in the conceptual tool-cabinet. . . . As adequacy criteria change, definitions usually develop in such a way that the definition complying with all the criteria becomes dominant.
>
> (P&R, p. 122, n. 1)

In other words, a theory that owes its appeal to a certain translation can be heuristically falsified if a better translation comes along. None of these 'translations' from less rigorous to more rigorous idioms preserve meanings exactly: they would be pointless if they did. The very merit of Epsilon/Poincaré's translation from geometry into algebra is that it does *not* quite preserve the old meanings, and the deformation that takes place is not just a random fuzziness, but a careful *development* of language which is simultaneously a theoretical advance.

In the last few pages of the dialogue, Epsilon appeals to the notion of the 'dominant theory', that is, the established vocabulary into which the old, vague discourse is translated. In the case of Poincaré/Epsilon's proof the dominant theory is set theory together with arithmetic. He claims that this dominant theory is *already* Euclidean, that it already has perfectly well understood terms and infallible inferences. Hence, by running the proof within this theory, he makes it infallible too. In other words, the theorem would be a necessary truth (or 'tautology', as Lakatos has it), relative to the dominant theory. That is to say, the validity of the proof would depend solely on the meanings of the terms of the dominant theory, and the theorem would be 'analytic' relative to that theory. Worrall and Zahar, in an extension to the dialogue, seem to argue that it makes a difference that we can make logic alone the dominant theory of mathematics. If logic is the dominant theory, runs the argument, then all our theorems can be logical 'tautologies', in that their proofs would only depend on the meanings of the logical terms. What is more, given any putative proof, we can check its validity in a finite number of steps. Hence, if we have no serious doubts about our logic, we can know that there are no logical counterexamples to the conditional statement: *given these premises, this conclusion follows*. Of course, we still have to wonder when our premises are true, if ever. Furthermore, the meta-theoretical results that assure us that our logic works are themselves informal, so there is always the possibility that one of these might come to be falsified.

There are therefore two points at which scepticism can be injected, according to Worrall and Zahar, in addition to the question of the adequacy of the translation into the formal idiom. However, a serious doubt about logic would be a serious doubt about thought itself. Hence, scepticism about the *if–then* result of the proof can only be idle philosophical mischief-making, and cannot be an argument for fallibilism in mathematics. Subject to the uncertainties of extracting an authorial view from a dialogue, the Worrall-Zahar position seems to be that translation into the idiom of formal logic effectively insulates a theorem from logical counterexamples and hence from serious doubt. Translation into logic is then the final moment in the life of a theorem; formal mathematics is fundamentally unlike informal mathematics, because the refutations characteristic of the latter are not possible in the former.

Worrall and Zahar are right up to a point. It is true that we are unlikely to have any serious doubts about logical rules such as *modus ponens*, but we can and do have doubts about the complex systems required for the expression of advanced mathematics. The more important objection, however, is that their addendum is off the point. During the discussion of concept-formation, Pi elucidated the difference between logical and heuristic counter-examples with the aid of a distinction: 'Heuristic is concerned with language-dynamics, while logic is concerned with language-statics' (P&R, p. 93). That is to say, a logical counterexample is one which defeats a conjecture within the present conceptual framework. A heuristic counterexample requires a (possibly covert) shift in meanings. However, significant advances in knowledge are always accompanied by conceptual change. Hence, by demanding a shift of meaning, a heuristic counterexample can act as an agent of progress.

To examine the possibility of logical refutation, as Worrall and Zahar do, is to engage in language statics. They are correct to observe that the possibility of a logical counterexample in a formal system is remote if we have checked its consistency with our best available methods. The worst that can happen to a consistent formal system is that it falls into disuse. This would seem to distinguish formal systems from the informal theories, which seemed to be defeated by direct counterexamples. However, the lesson of the discussion of concept-formation was that *none* of the informal theories were logically refuted. 'All interesting refutations are heuristic' (P&R, p. 93). That is, all the old versions of the conjecture were true within (some interpretations of) their original languages. The apparent 'refutations' were achieved with the aid of subtle and secret shifts of meaning. In other words, what happened to Euler's original conjecture was not logical refutation; rather, the theory of solids fell into disuse, and was eventually replaced by topology. Heuristics is the study of how and why bodies of theory fall into disuse, taking their associated conceptual networks with them. This is the difference between Lakatos and Popper in both mathematics and physical science. Popperian theories suffer refutation; Lakatosian theories and programmes suffer abandonment. Hence, neither Euler's original conjecture nor modern formal systems are seriously vulnerable to logical refutation, but both are vulnerable to heuristic falsification. That is, both are in danger of being left stranded by shifts in meaning which promise new theoretical benefits.

Of course, the original conjecture was brought down by direct (if subtle) changes in the meaning of a key term ('polyhedron'), whereas a formal system would be defeated by changes in the standards of adequacy of translation from informal to formal idioms. This only reflects the fact that in making the move from informal to formal language, there is an explicit process of translation, while the translation processes brought about by Alpha's early counterexamples were hidden in Delta's 'elucidations' until Pi drew attention to them. What is more, the unity of discovery and justification holds good at this level. Our confidence in any dominant theory as a vehicle for proof (i.e. justification) would be undermined by discoveries which either cast doubt on the dominant theory or which could not be expressed in it.[12] At the same time, the success of a putative dominant theory as a vehicle for discovery reinforces its claim to be a suitable idiom for proof.[13] Hence, there is nothing distinctive about logic as a dominant theory. Theorems in formal systems stand in danger of exactly the same kind of heuristic falsification as all the informal theorems in the dialogue. That is to say: Cauchy's proof is valid but irrelevant, because we now have better accounts of the phenomena in question. There is no reason why Poincaré/ Epsilon's proof should not eventually share that fate.

What, then, of simple formulae such as 1+2=3? Our second objection to fallibilism in mathematics was that truths such as these are so elementary that they cannot be open to serious doubt. Lakatos has Kappa argue that even these simple truths can be made defeasible by stretching the relevant terms. That much is obvious: if '+' changes its meaning then 1+2=3 may not be so self-evident. Crucially, Kappa argues that 'The whole story of algebra is a series of such concept- and proof-stretchings' (P&R, p. 102). In certain algebraic structures, it is not the case that 1+2=3 (in the ring of integers 0,1,2 for example). What is more, the numerals no longer mean what they used to. Jeremy Gray[14] argues that there was an ontological revolution in nineteenth-century mathematics; that 'although the objects of study were still superficially the same (numbers, curves, and so forth), the way they were regarded was entirely transformed'. He argues this claim in detail in two areas: algebraic number theory and geometry. In the former case, Gray shows how problems in number theory led to the invention of new kinds of numbers. This in turn brought about a revision of the concept of 'integer'. Previously, the extension of the concept 'integer' was restricted to the natural numbers and their negatives (the 'whole numbers' of elementary mathematics). By the end of the century:

The natural numbers 1,2,3 . . . and their negatives were now just one kind of integer among many. The term henceforth applied to any number-like object which could be said to be prime (or not), to divide another exactly (or not), and so forth.

(in Gillies 1992, p. 233)

In other words, 'integer' was now understood in such general terms that it could be applied in any algebraic structure with a multiplication operator. From being the name of a set of familiar objects it became a property understood in abstract terms. Gray describes a similar evolution in geometry, and sums up the development thus: 'foundational status transferred from the familiar (integer, straight line) to the abstract (the set, the axiom, the rule of inference)' (ibid., p. 246). The parts of this story most familiar to philosophers are the foundational efforts of logicians and set theorists. If formulae such as 1+2=3 were as simple as they look, Frege and Peano could not have bequeathed such knotty problems to their successors.

To put it another way: it has been and will remain the case that an apple taken together with two oranges makes three pieces of fruit. It is also the case that an apple released in mid-air will fall to earth. Nevertheless, in both cases the theoretical apparatus we use to describe and to account for the phenomenon is highly complex and open to criticism. Newton and Frege considered themselves to have produced true explanations of dynamics and arithmetic respectively, and the fate of their theories argues against dogmatism. Lakatos himself explained his epistemology of mathematics by comparing mathematics in general, and meta-mathematics in particular, with physical science, 'The logical theory of mathematics is an exciting, sophisticated speculation like any scientific theory' (vol. II, p. 19). According to Lakatos, truths can only be certain in so far as they are trivial, and only a perfectly trivial truth could be known with perfect certainty. Mathematics, being far from trivial, is far from certain.

Chapter 3

The Popper–Kuhn debate

In 1962 Thomas Kuhn published *The Structure of Scientific Revolutions*. The book caused a furore among philosophers of science, many of whom accused Kuhn of relativism and irrationalism (see Popper in Lakatos and Musgrave 1970, p. 56). Lakatos claimed that 'For Kuhn scientific change . . . is a mystical conversion which is not and cannot be governed by rules of reason and which falls totally within the realm of the *(social) psychology of discovery*' (Lakatos and Musgrave 1970, p. 93). Unfortunately for his critics, Kuhn originally trained as a physicist and was by then working as an historian of science. He was, therefore, rather difficult to dismiss as a crank. It is my view that much of the brouhaha depended upon a misreading of Kuhn. I shall not pursue that thought here, however, because the purpose of this chapter is to establish the context in which Lakatos developed his own views on the history and philosophy of science. As we shall see in the next chapter, Lakatos tried to emulate the historical sensitivity of Kuhn's work while avoiding what he saw as Kuhn's concessions to irrationalism. Hence, what we need is precisely Kuhn-as-read-by-Lakatos.

Kuhn's account of the emergence and development of mature science dispensed with many of the distinctions and definitions which his empiricist and Popperian predecessors regarded as essential to any grasp of objectivity and rationality. In particular, he had no use for the distinction between the contexts of discovery and justification:

> My attempts to apply [these distinctions] even *grosso modo*, to the actual situations in which knowledge is gained, accepted, and assimilated have made them seem extraordinarily problematic.

Rather than being elementary logical or methodological distinctions, which would then be prior to the analysis of scientific knowledge, they now seem to be integral parts of a traditional set of substantive answers to the very questions upon which they have been deployed.

(SSR, p. 9)

Kuhn does not, in these programmatic remarks, claim that the old philosophical distinctions are incoherent or pernicious. All he suggests is that they are not as fundamental as had hitherto been thought, and that their importance could be tested with the aid of the history of science.

Kuhn's picture of the scientific enterprise invokes distinctions of his own making, the first of which is between immature and mature fields of scientific research. An immature field is marked by the existence of many rival schools. Since no single approach dominates, practitioners are free to choose whatever metaphysical or methodological principles they wish. The price of this freedom is that, when writing up his work, the scientist in an immature field can take nothing for granted. Since there is no common body of belief, each writer must argue from (and indeed for) first principles. Consequently, scientists in immature fields are compelled to engage in metaphysical and methodological debate with rival schools. It is difficult, under these conditions, for scientists to explore the detailed consequences of their own theoretical commitments. It is still more difficult to establish the situation typical of mature disciplines in which a single cluster of ideas is pursued in many independent research centres. Scientists typically amass plenty of empirical information during this immature phase, but this fact-gathering activity is almost random because there is no agreed framework to distinguish important data from mere curiosities. Consequently, however brilliant and rigorous individuals may be in their thinking, the net result of work in an immature discipline is, says Kuhn, 'something less than science' (SSR, p. 13).

The field achieves maturity when these disparate efforts unite around a single conception of what the important questions are, what methods are appropriate for their investigation and what would count as an acceptable answer. In Kuhn's view this unity is not achieved by the discovery of any decisive metaphysical or methodological argument. Rather, the field comes together when someone produces a work with two crucial features. First, it must be sufficiently striking and impressive to attract an 'enduring group' (SSR, p. 10) of scientists away from rival scientific approaches. Second, it must be sufficiently open-ended to leave plenty for its adherents to do. In other words, the unifying work must be both compelling and suggestive. Kuhn offers as examples Aristotle's *Physica*, Ptolemy's *Almagest*, Newton's *Principia* and *Opticks*, Franklin's *Electricity*, Lavoisier's *Chemistry* and Lyell's *Geology*. Works such as these which implicitly 'define the legitimate problems and methods of a research field' Kuhn calls 'paradigms'. His claim is that the coherence of a mature science is due to the shared admiration of scientists for some *paradigmatic* example of good work in the field, and their determination to produce more of the same.

Unfortunately, Kuhn's use of the word 'paradigm' in *The Structure of Scientific Revolutions* is rather loose. At times, he uses it to mean *both* the unifying treatise (the *Physica* or *Opticks*) *and* that which the scientists share in virtue of their common admiration for it. Thus, the 'Newtonian paradigm' could mean both the *Opticks* itself or the 'Newtonianism' of those who tried to extend and develop it (or both). Subsequently, Kuhn has endeavoured to clear up this unfortunate ambiguity, and has introduced the expression 'disciplinary matrix' to refer to the 'Newtonianism' (or 'Aristotelianism', etc.) arising from the shared admiration of scientists for the paradigmatic work in question.[1]

At any rate, once a paradigm is established, it provides a worked example and a range of problems for scientists to attack. Part of what it means to belong to a discipline defined by a paradigm is to believe that these problems will yield to solutions similar to those in the paradigmatic work. This task of extending and developing the themes initiated by that work is called, by Kuhn, 'normal science'. For Kuhn, almost all scientific activity is of this lead-following sort. The only exception is when the normal science stemming from a paradigm suffers a crisis. Then, the discipline enters a phase similar to its immature period, until a new paradigm emerges to unify the discipline again. These exceptional episodes are Kuhn's 'scientific revolutions'.

Criticisms of Kuhn's account of the scientific process concentrated on four of its features:

1 the 'gestalt-switch' character of the conversion of scientists
   from an old paradigm to a new one;
2 the incommensurability thesis;
3 the alleged relativism; *and*
4 the uncritical nature of Kuhnian normal science.

On the first point, Kuhn argued in *The Structure of Scientific
Revolutions* that the transition from one paradigm to the next is
like, if not actually a case of, a 'gestalt switch'. This phenomenon
results from experiments in psychology which relate our percep-
tions to our expectations. The simplest case is the duck-rabbit, a
line drawing which may initially strike the observer either as a
duck or as a rabbit.[2] The 'gestalt switch' is the rapid shift from
perceiving a duck to perceiving a rabbit. Kuhn's favourite
example is a rather more complicated experiment using playing
cards (SSR, pp. 62–4, 114). In this experiment, subjects are asked
to identify cards which they are shown for brief, measured
periods of time. Some of the cards are non-standard, for example
there may be a red six of clubs. At short exposures (which are
still long enough for most of the normal cards to be correctly
identified) the subjects do not notice that any of the cards are
odd. At slightly longer exposure times, the subjects report confusion and unease. It normally takes a long time before subjects are
able to explain their discomfort by correctly describing the
anomalous cards. To do that, they have to stop seeing the cards
as ordinary playing cards. They must undergo a gestalt switch.

Kuhn's claim is that this process is similar to (if not identical
with) the transition from one paradigm to another. For example
(SSR, p. 116) the Chinese, according to Kuhn, did not share the
early European conviction that the heavens are immutable.
Consequently they were able to see and record the appearance of
new stars which were invisible to western astronomers. A new
star, for European astronomers, was like a red six of clubs. They
didn't see it because they had a set of expectations which
convinced them that such a thing is impossible.

This 'gestalt switch' view of scientific revolutions is clearly
incompatible with the sort of empiricist philosophy of science
which builds its account of scientific objectivity on the notion of
theory-neutral observation. It also presents a difficulty for
philosophers (in any tradition) hoping to produce a general logic
of science. This aspiration depends on the idea that the replace-

ment of an old theory by a new one is achieved by following an explicit logical method. In this case, scientists should be driven by the force of argument from the old view to the new one. On Kuhn's view, however, the change is not logically compelling. If enough scientists fall into the grip of the new gestalt then a revolution will take place. In any case, responsibility for explaining changes in scientific orthodoxy seems to have passed from philosophers and logicians to psychologists and sociologists.

The fear that Kuhnian paradigm-shifts are unreasoned is exacerbated by the analogy between scientific and political revolutions. A political revolution happens, according to Kuhn, when society becomes polarised between those who hope to maintain and improve the existing institutions and those who hope to replace them:

> Because they differ about the institutional matrix within which political change is to be achieved and evaluated, because they acknowledge no supra-institutional framework for the adjudication of revolutionary difference, the parties to a revolutionary conflict must finally resort to the techniques of mass persuasion, often including force.
>
> (SSR, p. 93)

Similarly, a competition between paradigms cannot be settled by following some agreed procedure because the competing camps disagree over the detail of what is to count as a properly scientific approach. 'As in political revolutions, so in paradigm choice, there is no standard higher than the assent of the relevant community' (SSR, p. 96). To imagine the effect of these passages on Lakatos, recall that he had seen 'the techniques of mass persuasion, often including force' at work during his life in Hungary. Part of the attraction of Popper's philosophy for him was that according to Popper there *is* a universal standard of rationality. Political and scientific differences need never be settled by physical or rhetorical force, in Popper's view, because disputants can always bring their claims to the court of reason. If, on the other hand, there is no universal and impartial rationality then scientists (and political activists) can argue that they are compelled to use 'whatever means necessary' to advance their views (just as, in the absence of an impartial police force and justice system, the most peaceful person may be forced to become a vigilante).

It might be thought that, even if during a scientific revolution logic temporarily gives way to charisma and chicanery, it is nevertheless possible to judge after the event whether the paradigm shift was a genuine advance. Such retrospective judgments are not always possible, according to Kuhn, because successive paradigms are sometimes *incommensurable*. What this means is that a new paradigm brings new concepts and, crucially, new standards of evaluation for theories. In Aristotelian physics, a stone falls because it is in its nature to seek the centre of the universe. This, for the medieval scholastic philosophers, was a perfectly good, scientific explanation. By Newton's time, Aristotelian physics had given way to a corpuscularian outlook, according to which all phenomena were to be explained 'in terms of the size, shape, position and motion of elementary corpuscles of base matter' (SSR, p. 104). Explanations in the Aristotelian tradition were viewed as unscientific verbal flummery – to say that a body falls because it has a tendency to fall is no explanation at all. Thus, the new corpuscularian metaphysics introduced new standards of scientific practice as well as new theories and problems.

The triumph was relatively short-lived, however, because Newton's *Principia* treated gravity as an innate attraction between bodies (that is, as a basic property of matter not reducible to size, shape, position and motion). This innate gravitational attraction cannot itself be detected by the senses (though its effects can). In other words, Newton's gravity was just as much an occult (hidden) property as any Aristotelian essence. In spite of heroic efforts, it was not possible to reconcile the *Principia* with corpuscularian standards and scientists were eventually forced to admit that some phenomena at least are best explained, scientifically, by appeal to occult properties. Thus, by the standards of his immediate predecessors, Newton's work was unscientific. On the other hand, within the disciplinary matrix established by Newton's paradigmatic works the theory of gravity was the leading example of good scientific work.

In general, the incommensurability thesis seems to claim that there is no universal yardstick against which scientific explanations can be measured and compared because sometimes a paradigm-shift introduces a whole new conception of what it is to be scientific. By corpuscularian standards, scholastic explanations are little more than tautologies. By Aristotelian standards, corpuscularian explanations are at best incomplete since they typically fail to identify the final cause (the purpose, the *telos*) of the phenomenon to be explained. Consequently, if Kuhn is right, it is not always possible to judge whether a given scientific revolution is an improvement in knowledge without arbitrarily privileging one set of standards over the other. Certainly, there is no timeless formula for calculating the relative merits of scientific theories.

Still worse, from the point of view of Kuhn's philosophical critics, is his account of progress. Kuhn does think that progress in science is possible. He holds that 'the nature of [scientific] communities provides a virtual guarantee that both the list of problems solved by science and the precision of individual problem-solutions will continue to grow' (SSR, p. 170). What he does not offer is progress towards truth. His task is to understand the existence and success of science, and he doubts that it helps to suppose that 'there is some one full, objective, true account of nature and that the proper measure of scientific achievement is the extent to which it brings us closer to that ultimate goal' (SSR, p. 171). This, to many philosophers, sounds like relativism. Given two paradigms Kuhn may allow us to say that one solves more problems more precisely than the other. What Kuhn has no use for is the suggestion that one is 'more true' (has greater verisimilitude) than the other.

What was perhaps the most worrying feature of *The Structure of Scientific Revolutions* for Popperian philosophers was Kuhn's description of 'normal science'. On Kuhn's view, scientists almost never ask fundamental questions. What they do is to solve puzzles thrown up by whatever paradigmatic work it was that created the given field. Kuhn chose the word 'puzzle' carefully. In doing a crossword puzzle, one knows that there is a solution, that it will be of a certain familiar sort and that it will bear the usual kind of relationship with the clues. The normal scientist regards his work in a similar light, for the paradigm tells him that his problems have solutions of a closely-specified sort. This is not to deny that scientific puzzles are typically rather more complex and taxing than crosswords, and sometimes require enormous skill and ingenuity. Kuhnian normal science is, nevertheless, uncritical:

[it] seems an attempt to force nature into the preformed and relatively inflexible box that the paradigm supplies. No part of the aim of normal science is to call forth new sorts of phenomena; indeed those that will not fit the box are often not seen at all. Nor do scientists normally aim to invent new theories, and they are often intolerant of those invented by others.

(SSR, p. 24)

There could hardly be a greater contrast with the image of science advanced by Popper. Popperian scientists spend most of their time trying to disprove the scientific orthodoxies of the day. On Popper's view one would expect to find scientists designing experiments to bring new phenomena to light (in the hope that these phenomena will turn out to be counterexamples to the presently accepted theories). Far from ignoring awkward evidence the Popperian scientist sets out expressly to find cases that will not fit in the current 'preformed and relatively inflexible box'. When a theory is found to be false, the Popperian scientist invents a new one, and is always open to theories invented by others. Popperian scientists are nothing if not critical.

Kuhn's picture of normal scientists uncritically labouring in the service of the dominant paradigm was, in Popper's view, the most dangerous aspect of *The Structure of Scientific Revolutions*. If there are any Kuhnian normal scientists then, thought Popper, they are to be pitied: 'The "normal scientist", as described by Kuhn, has been badly taught. He has been taught in a dogmatic spirit: he is a victim of indoctrination' (Lakatos and Musgrave, p. 53).

Kuhn, for his part, did not altogether dispute this description of the normal scientist. He observed that scientists in training do not read the works of their great dead predecessors, as philosophers do. Science students read recently-written textbooks. If the history of the discipline appears at all in these works, it is purged of revolutions. Students are encouraged to think that the present conception of what it is to be scientific has always prevailed and was shared by their heroes. This is achieved by censorship, 'When it repudiates a past paradigm, a scientific community simultaneously renounces, as a fit subject for professional scrutiny, most of the books and articles in which that paradigm had been embodied' (SSR, p. 167).

The important difference between Popper and Kuhn here is that while Popper vehemently denied that censorship has any place in science, Kuhn thought that the logic of science requires that students should be brainwashed into thinking that current standards and practices are universal criteria of scientific rationality. Normal science is the engine of progress, but normal science is only possible so long as fundamental questions are assumed to have been permanently settled at some unspecified time in the historic past. Hence, progress requires uncritical acceptance of present orthodoxies bolstered by a systematic distortion of the past. Kuhn was aware of the political significance of this line of thought, 'the member of a mature scientific community is, like the typical character of Orwell's *1984*, the victim of a history rewritten by the powers that be' (SSR, p. 167).

Popper was appalled by Kuhn's insistence that normal scientists are uncritical puzzle-solvers because criticism is the unifying theme of his entire life's work, from *The Logic of Scientific Discovery* to *The Open Society and its Enemies*. For Popper, science progresses through the critical testing of theories. The scientific community is scientific precisely because it is a society of mutual critics. On the other hand, 'open' societies are defined as those in which criticism is possible because speech is free. A virtuous society is one which tolerates and even encourages dissenting opinion. For Popper, the scientific community is the finest example of a virtuous open society. Indeed, if it ceased to be an open society, it would cease to be scientific. Hence, Popper's account of science is also his argument for political freedom. By suggesting that the logic of science requires a kind of Stalinism, Kuhn seemed to be offering intellectual comfort to despots.

On the one hand, Lakatos shared Popper's conviction that Kuhn's account of science is politically dangerous:

> The clash between Popper and Kuhn is not about a mere technical point in epistemology. It concerns our central intellectual values, and has implications not only for theoretical physics but also for the underdeveloped social sciences and even for moral and political philosophy.
>
> (vol. I, p. 9)

On the other hand, Lakatos agreed with Kuhn that the rationalist accounts of science then available bore little relation to the activities of real scientists. The only solution to this dilemma was to develop a theory of scientific method which was sufficiently subtle to cope with the detail of the actual history of science and yet sufficiently rationalistic to resist the political dangers presented by Kuhn. Lakatos' attempt to develop a theory to meet this need is the subject of the next chapter.

Chapter 4

Philosophy of science

The central issue for Popperian philosophy of science was the *demarcation problem*: how can genuine science be distinguished from pseudo-science? Popper thought that truly scientific disciplines (such as physics) must share some common feature which is lacking in what he considered to be pseudo-sciences (such as psychoanalytic theory). Moreover, this common element must be something to do with the logical structure of the theories found in genuine sciences. Therefore, the demarcation problem is the quest for the logical feature peculiar to scientific theories. In Popper's view, the distinctive logical fact about science is that its theories can be tested against empirical evidence. If a physical theory, for example, makes a prediction which turns out to be false, then the theory itself must be false. Psychoanalytic theory, on the other hand, cannot be empirically falsified because it is compatible with any empirical data whatsoever (so Popper argued).

In the case of Marxism (another pseudo-scientific theory in Popper's view), the diagnosis is a little more complicated.[1] Marx's philosophy made testable predictions (e.g. that revolution would happen first in the most technologically advanced countries). When these predictions turned out to be false, Popper thought, Marx's followers ought to have abandoned his theory. Instead, many of them tried to rescue the theory by adjusting and reinterpreting it. These running repairs may have saved it from falsification, but they did so at a price. Popper defined the empirical content of a theory as the range of possible circumstances that the theory rules out. The remarkable thing about our best scientific theories, according to Popper, is that they are incompatible with a vast range of possible circumstances, yet they remain (so far) unfalsified. By arguing that Marxism is not incompatible with the facts of history, its defenders saved it by reducing its empirical content. Hence, a scientific discipline, for Popper, is one which does not use *ad hoc* manoeuvres (or 'conventionalist stratagems') to preserve its theories from refutation at the expense of their empirical content. Part of what it means for science to progress is that when an old theory is replaced by a new one, the new theory should have at least as much empirical content (so defined) as its predecessor. Notice that in this case, the criticism is not aimed at a single theory, but rather at a series of theories. The Popperian complaint is that each successive formulation of the central Marxist idea had less empirical content than its predecessor.

Popper's entire career as a philosopher of science was dedicated to the technical development of his proposed solution to the demarcation problem and to philosophical issues arising from it. As a student of Popper, Lakatos treated the recent history of philosophy of science as a catalogue of attempts to solve the demarcation problem, the chief of which (in his view) were *inductivism, conventionalism* and Popper's *methodological falsificationism*. For 'inductivists', proper science means proving theories from observed facts by means of a rigorous 'logic of induction'. For so-called 'conventionalists', proper science means constructing the simplest taxonomy of phenomena which saves appearances. The theories thus produced are 'true by convention', because their acceptance is based not only on empirical criteria but also on our preference for simple theories. For 'methodological falsificationists', proper science means inventing testable theories, and then testing them. (It is of course debatable how many of Lakatos' predecessors would recognise themselves in this taxonomy.)

The proliferation of putative solutions to the demarcation problem raises a new difficulty. Genuine science strives for proven theories, or simple theories, or falsifiable-but-unfalsified theories, depending on the choice of demarcation criterion. Given this range of demarcation criteria (and there are, of course, many variations on each theme), we have to ask, how is one to adjudicate among them? On what grounds might we select one definition of science ahead of the rest? Lakatos' answer is: by appeal to history.

Each definition of proper science divides history into rational

episodes and non-rational episodes. A rational episode is one
which fulfils whichever criterion of science happens to be in
hand. For an inductivist, for example, the rational episodes in the
history of science are those which conform to the 'logic of induction'. Theories accepted on other occasions are mere pseudo-
science. Now, we already have views about the history of
science, in advance of our philosophical investigation of the
demarcation problem. We believe that it was rational for physicists to choose Einstein over Newton, to cite a well-worn
example, and on the whole we believe that we are rational to
accept our present set of theories in most of the mature sciences
at least. These beliefs about the history of science provide a
bedrock of basic data against which to test solutions to the
demarcation problem. If a criterion of 'proper' (i.e. rational)
science sorts the history into rational and non-rational episodes
in a way which brands many of our most cherished scientific
successes as non-rational, then there is probably something
wrong with it. This method of finding a philosophy to fit established views about what is or is not good science was explicit in
Lakatos, but he learned it from Popper, who had no doubts
about where Freud and Marx should find themselves when the
line separating science from pseudo-science is drawn (cf. vol. I,
p. 153, n. 2).

It was Lakatos' view that inductivism, conventionalism and
methodological falsificationism all collapse when exposed to the
tribunal of history. When the archives are examined, it turns out
that there never was a 'logic of induction', and historical figures
such as Newton who claimed (according to Lakatos) to derive
their theories inductively from bare phenomena were in fact
doing something else entirely (cf. vol. I, p. 210). Hence, if inductivism really does provide the criterion for scientific (i.e. rational)
inquiry, then almost the entire history of science is a tale of unscientific, irrational superstition. For Lakatos, inductivism requires
such an extensive distortion of the past, and inverts our views of
historical success and failure so comprehensively, that it cannot
be right. A similar argument is made against conventionalism.
Copernicus is said to have claimed that his theory is better than
that of Ptolemy because it is simpler. According to Lakatos:

> The [Copernican] system is simpler in so far as it leaves the
> eighth sphere of fixed stars immobile and removes its two

Ptolemaic motions; but Copernicus has to pay for the immo-bile eighth sphere by transferring its irregular Ptolemaic movements to the already corrupt earth which Copernicus sets spinning with a rather complicated wobble; he also has to put the centre of the universe, not at the Sun, as he originally intended, but at an empty point fairly near to it.

(vol. I, p. 174)

Consequently, says Lakatos, 'the simplicity balance between Ptolemy's and Copernicus' system is roughly even'. Therefore 'If dramatic increase in simplicity of observationally equivalent theories is the hallmark of scientific revolution, the Copernican Revolution cannot be regarded as one' (ibid.).

Finally, falsificationism falls to the same line of attack. For falsificationists, the history of science is a sequence of daring speculations and 'crucial experiments', that is, experiments which falsify leading theories. The trouble here is that, on Lakatos' view, every great scientific theory in history has been engulfed in an 'ocean of anomalies' from the moment of its formulation (cf. vol. I, p. 172). That is, all great theories are born falsified. According to falsificationist methodology, it is irrational to persist with a falsified theory. It follows that if falsificationism is true, then none of the great scientific success stories is properly scientific. Falsificationism therefore overthrows all of our judge-ments of scientific success. What is more, it cannot explain why some falsifying experiments are viewed with hindsight as 'crucial' while others (the vast majority) are not. Falsificationists need to distort history because they need to find a 'crucial exper-iment' whenever a theory is rationally discarded.[2]

THE METHODOLOGY OF SCIENTIFIC RESEARCH PROGRAMMES

If none of the leading demarcation criteria can survive the tribunal of history, then what distinction can be made between science and non-science? Lakatos' attempt to solve the problem is his *methodology of scientific research programmes*. In the first place, he claims that the appropriate unit of appraisal is not the individual theory (and certainly not the individual proposition). Instead, we ought to examine sequences of historically related theories. To see why, consider Popper's original thought that if a theory is falsified then one either does the decent thing and abandons it, or one turns away from science. Most Marxists (for example) showed themselves to be unscientific (in Popper's eyes) by remaining Marxists when their theory was falsified. They were able to do this because there are always 'conventionalist stratagems' available. That is, they were able to protect the central tenets of Marxism by adjusting and reinterpreting details on the periphery of the theory, at the cost of reducing its empirical content. The example suggests a rule: one should develop a central idea in such a way that modifications should not decrease its empirical content. More generally, this line of thought implies that what makes for scientific respectability is the manner in which one develops and nurtures a cluster of thoughts over time, rather than any purely logical feature.

Popper never succeeded in incorporating this insight into his philosophical theory. The reason, Lakatos thought, was that Popper remained committed to the theory as the unit of appraisal (cf. vol. I, p. 34, n. 5). Theories are static in the sense that their content does not change over time, for to change the content of a theory is (strictly speaking) to produce a new theory. In order to capture the thought of the previous paragraph, we require a unit of scientific appraisal which can maintain its identity as it changes. Lakatos' suggestion for this role is the 'research programme'. In his sense, a research programme is the sum of the various stages through which a leading idea passes. This 'leading idea' provides the 'hard core' of the research programme, that is, a set of commitments which cannot be abandoned without abandoning the research programme altogether. Lakatos offers as an example the three laws of motion and the law of gravitation as the hard core of Newton's research programme (vol. I, p. 179). The existence of such 'hard cores' at the heart of the most scientific of research programmes seems to have grown from reflection on a remark of Popper's: Popper demanded that a scientist ought to be able to say under what conditions he would abandon his theory (if there are no such conditions then by Popper's lights the theory is unfalsifiable and hence unscientific). Lakatos realised that if that question had been put to Newtonian physicists in the heyday of the Newtonian research programme, they would have been just as nonplussed as any Marxist or Freudian (vol. I, p. 147). The reason is that Newtonians (and other scientists) are no more prepared to put the central tenets of their belief-systems up for grabs than anyone else. One way of drawing the distinction is this: Popper claimed that what distinguished his philosophy of science from 'conventionalism' is that in his view only highly particular 'basic statements' can be conventional, whereas for conventionalists, any part of the theory can be regarded as conventional, including its most general propositions. Lakatos sided against Popper by recognising the unfalsifiable 'hard core' at the heart of every scientific research programme (cf. vol. I, p. 148).

In addition to the 'hard core' of commitments of the research programme, there is a 'protective belt' of auxiliary hypotheses which shields the hard core from falsification. Lakatos either borrowed or reinvented the Quinean thought that one can always protect a cherished belief from hostile evidence by redirecting the criticism towards other elements of the belief system.[3] In Lakatos' model, criticism is deflected away from the hard core towards the protective belt. In Newton's programme, for example, this role was played by (amongst other things) geometrical optics and Newton's theory of atmospheric refraction (vol. I, p. 179). If the observed movements of heavenly bodies seemed not to accord with the predictions of Newton's core theory, then the observations must be distorted by the atmosphere or misinterpreted by poor optical theory.

Hence, the belt of auxiliary hypotheses is constantly changing, partly in response to empirical developments, but hopefully also under the guidance of the programme's 'heuristic' (that is, its collection of characteristic problem-solving techniques). As we saw in Chapter 2, the word 'heuristic' underwent considerable development in Lakatos' thought, starting with a simple sense borrowed from George Pólya. To reiterate: in *Proofs and Refutations*, the word grew out of its Pólya-sense and came to mean the general theory of rational change from one stage of a conjecture to the next (cf. P&R, p. 93). Now, Popper distinguished between the psychology of conjecture-production and the logic of appraisal. That is to say, he thought that the formulation of hypotheses was a problem for psychology and sociology, while the evaluation and testing of hypotheses is a problem for logic. The work of Pólya convinced Lakatos that there is more to say on the production of conjectures than this, and that rational procedures can be followed (even if, as Pólya stressed, there is no guarantee of success) (vol. I, p. 140). Lakatos learned from Pólya that there can be a *logic* of mathematical conjecture-production and then, in *Proofs and Refutations*, went on to break down the distinction between the logic of invention (as explored by Pólya) and the logic of evaluation (as investigated by Popper). By the closing pages of *Proofs and Refutations*, 'heuristics' had come to denote the general theory of rational mathematical practice.

In later work on the general philosophy of science, the distinction between invention and appraisal was superseded by a new distinction between 'methodology' and 'heuristics', through which both these words developed new meanings. A *methodology* in this sense is a solution to Popper's demarcation question, that is, a specification of the logical features characteristic of science. A *heuristic* is a set of problem-solving techniques for scientists engaged in a particular research programme. Lakatos explained the difference with an analogy (which he credits to John Watkins): 'Methodology is separated from *heuristics* rather as value judgments are from "ought" statements' (vol. I, p. 103, n. 1). The fact that 'methodology' is a rather inaccurate word for the job merely reflects the fact that earlier philosophers of science had mostly failed to separate the demarcation question from the question of how scientists should behave. To continue Lakatos' example, the heuristic of Newton's programme chiefly consisted in its mathematical apparatus: the differential calculus, the theory of convergence and differential and integral equations.

An important difference between *Proofs and Refutations* and the papers on the methodology of scientific research programmes is that in the latter, a 'heuristic' is specific to a particular programme. Instead of a single general body of good research advice (such as was supplied by Pólya), heuristics became that part of the programme which tells scientists in that particular programme how to go on. Indeed, it is not normally possible to identify a heuristic separately from the programme of which it is a part. This point is important because the conception of a heuristic being tied to a research programme is integral to Lakatos' proposed solution to the demarcation problem. The central idea of his solution is this: the history of science is one of extended wars of attrition between research programmes, some of which are 'progressing', while others are 'degenerating'. A discipline is scientific so long as progressive programmes triumph over degenerating ones.

This thought clearly requires an account of what it is for a programme to progress. For Lakatos, change comes to a progressive programme from its own inner logic, whereas a degenerating programme changes in response to external criticism. The example he had in mind was Newton:

> Newton first worked out his programme for a planetary system with a fixed point-like sun and one single point-like planet. It was in this model that he derived his inverse square law for Kepler's ellipse. But this model was forbidden by Newton's own third law of dynamics, therefore the model had to be replaced by one in which both sun and planet revolved round their common centre of gravity. . . . Then he worked out the programme for more planets as if there were only heliocentric but no interplanetary forces. Then he worked out the case where the sun and planets were not mass-points but mass-*balls*. . . . Having solved this 'puzzle', he started work on *spinning balls* and their wobbles. Then he admitted interplanetary forces and started work on *perturbations*.
>
> (vol. I, p. 50)

This is the paradigmatic research programme: a sequence of theories representing stages in the development of a central idea. The important point is that the successive modifications were not forced on Newton by awkward empirical facts. Indeed, Newton scarcely glanced at the facts at all. Rather, the modifications were prompted by internal logical problems (such as the inadmissibility of infinite density in Newton's system) which were solved using the programme's heuristic (i.e. Newtonian mathematics). Newton was able to ignore the fact that none of these models was empirically adequate because the programme held out the promise that if he continued in the same vein he would eventually produce a model which would not only respect the empirical evidence but also explain it.

Thus, in a progressive research programme the central idea is developed and refined using the resources of the heuristic. Anomalies can and should be ignored in the hope that they will be accommodated and explained by a later stage of the programme. That hope evaporates when the heuristic encounters problems which it cannot solve. Then, the programme enters a degenerating phase, marked by *ad hoc* efforts to protect the hard core from criticism with the aid of devices external to the programme. So long as successive changes to the protective belt of auxiliary hypotheses are 'in the spirit of the heuristic' (vol. I, p. 179) the programme is said to make *heuristic progress*.

Heuristic progress alone is not enough, however. A progressive programme may ignore its anomalies, but it must also make *empirical progress*. Empirically progressive programmes predict facts which are not only new but undreamed of,[4] and it is especially good if the predicted facts are counterexamples to rival programmes. Lakatos' favourite example was that of Einstein's theory, which predicted that the distance measured between two stars would vary according to the time of day. The discovery is a powerful indication of the productivity of Einstein's programme because it is unlikely that anyone would have thought to make the measurement otherwise. Einstein gets as much credit for suggesting the experiment as he does for getting the prediction right (vol. I, p. 5). In general, a programme is *theoretically progressive* if modifications lead to unexpected predictions, and it is *empirically progressive* if some of these are corroborated.

This, in outline, is Lakatos' solution to the demarcation problem. Notice that the definition of heuristic progress is in fact a schema which gives a different specification for each programme. Modifications to a programme must be driven by its heuristic, but the meaning of this formula depends on the programme in hand. Thus, the 'heuristic' of a programme plays a double role: it provides a logic of discovery for the scientists working on the programme, and at the same time sets the standard by which the programme is to be evaluated (since fidelity to the 'spirit of its heuristic' is a criterion of progress in a programme).

What emerges is a very different picture of 'healthy science' from that offered by Popper. To begin with, a healthy research programme is driven not by refutations, but principally by its heuristic. So long as there are some 'dramatic' empirical results, and a steady supply of the kind of problem for which the techniques of the heuristic are effective, then the programme can ignore anomalies. It is only when the heuristic runs out of steam that the anomalies have to be taken seriously. Of course, scientists do not like to be accused of ignoring 'the facts'. We can therefore expect to find that when a research programme is vigorous, scientists indulge in logical conjuring tricks which allow them to ignore anomalies without seeming to ignore logic. A standard device is the re-flagging of anomalies as 'exceptions'.

One merely makes a list of them and tacks it on to the end of the theory in question. Lakatos reports that there were plenty of places at which Newton's astronomy was at variance with the facts (vol. I, pp. 50 and 215), but the Newtonians regarded these anomalies not as refutations but as ongoing problems, and had no doubt that their programme would deal with these puzzles eventually. Now, according to Popperian methodology, the Newtonians were straying from the path. As good scientists, they ought to have abandoned their theory immediately on discovering the anomalies. For Lakatos, on the other hand, it was entirely rational for the Newtonians to press on because they had good grounds for confidence in the heuristic of their programme. To abandon a progressive programme over a few details would have been a terrible waste. What is more, it would not have made the programme one whit more progressive to have cobbled together some *ad hoc* explanation of the anomalies. Indeed, it would have signalled the beginning of a degenerative phase. Far better to make a list of problems and hope that the programme can eventually digest them naturally. Hence, the concept of a heuristically-driven programme explains why famously competent scientists sometimes seem to take a cavalier attitude to anomalies, and in general it explains the relative autonomy of theory, because we can see how in a heuristically-driven programme there can be times when theory surges ahead of experimentation (cf. vol. I, p. 149). What is more, the methodology of scientific research programmes predicts that there may well be some kind of exception-barring going on in the early vigorous stage of any research programme. For Lakatos, it is both predictable and rational that scientists should protect a progressive programme from carping criticism.[5]

Another significant difference between Lakatosian and Popperian 'good science' is that for Lakatos, it is impossible to award prizes until the dust settles. It is only after a long struggle that one research programme can triumph over another by showing the extra productivity of its heuristic. Even then, there can be no absolute certainty that the exhausted heuristic of the defeated programme might not be rejuvenated somehow. When the work is actually being done there is no way of knowing how successful a programme is going to be in digesting anomalies, and hence there is no way of sorting really damaging refutations from mere problems-to-solve. Of course, after the event it is possible to point to the anomalies which proved indigestible (within the terms of the heuristic) and to label them as 'crucial experiments' (i.e. theory-refuting experiments). This, however, is the wisdom of hindsight. Lakatos' demarcation criterion is in this sense less strict than Popper's, because it allows scientists to keep on with an inconsistent programme and to leave the appraisal of the whole programme to posterity. An immediate consequence is that, 'The old rationalist dream of a mechanical, semi-mechanical or at least fast-acting method for showing up falsehood, unprovenness, meaningless rubbish or even non-rational choice has to be given up' (vol. I, p. 149). Lakatos sometimes put his point in this way: the mark of the scientist is not whether he abandons his theory in the face of a counterexample, but how he advances to the next stage of his research programme (of course, there may be times when it is rational to abandon the research programme), and this point separates the question of appraisal from the question of rejection. That is, the question 'when ought I to abandon my theory?' has been separated from the question 'is this inquiry genuinely scientific?' In Popper, these questions are identical (cf. vol. I, p. 150), because for Popper a theory is scientific only if its champions are prepared to abandon it when it is falsified. For Lakatos, an inquiry is 'scientific' if it can be written up afterwards as meeting the standards of the methodology of scientific research programmes, but a programme may only be abandoned if there is a manifestly better alternative available. Hence, Lakatos makes more sense than Popper out of the fact that when all the available theories in some field are deeply flawed, scientists hang on to their least lousy theory in spite of its shortcomings.[6]

STATUTE AND CASE LAW

Lakatos was committed to the possibility of a universal conception of scientific progress while at the same time denying the possibility of 'mechanical' or 'fast-acting' rationality. There is a tension here, because a truly universal criterion of the scientific would be a rule which could be applied without having to be interpreted differently for different programmes, but that sounds like 'mechanical' rationality (even if it were not 'fast-acting'). Lakatos was aware that there is at best a trade-off here, and he sometimes put the point by means of a legal analogy. He contrasts philosophers of science (such as Popper) who hope to produce a demarcation criterion by *a priori* means with 'élitists' who maintain that philosophers can have nothing useful to add to the intuitive judgement of leading scientists when it comes to the evaluation of scientific work. The former group holds that 'there must be the constitutional authority of an *immutable statute law* (laid down in [a] demarcation criterion) to distinguish between good and bad science' (vol. I, p. 136). This, says Lakatos, is sheer *hubris* since it requires the work of great scientists to be judged according to standards developed from the philosopher's armchair. On the other hand, he also disagrees with philosophers of the latter group who hold that 'there must be, and can be, no statute law at all: only case law', that is, that top scientists must make a separate intuitive decision for every case. Part of the problem is that both these views tacitly suppose that scientific rationality is found by means of an inner light of reason, since neither explains from where else the judgements might spring. The apriorist is a kind of subjectivist because he grounds his statute law in some apparently self-evident logical principles which can only reflect the workings of his own consciousness. Meanwhile the 'élitist' decides individual cases by means of an equally subjective 'intuition'.

Lakatos held that statute law and case law should inform each other, and he hoped thereby to avoid the subjectivism of the two extreme positions. Scientific statute law is formed, not by excogitation, but by the systematic articulation of the wisdom of scientific juries. On the other hand, scientific case law is always developed in the light of some general conception of 'good work in the field', however nebulous or implicit. After all, the judgement of the scientific aristocracy is only important because these leading scientists have the appropriate training and experience. There must be some systematic logical connection between their qualifications and the particular evaluation in hand. The fact that Lakatos understood the philosophy of science to be a reasoned exchange between philosophical theory and scientific practice may explain why some philosophers have had difficulty in grasping his arguments. Rather than stating premises and deducing their consequences, Lakatos shuttles back and forth between scientific cases and methodological statutes.

THE METHODOLOGY OF HISTORICAL RESEARCH PROGRAMMES

Lakatos developed the methodology of scientific research programmes by applying Popperian standards to Popper himself. When asked, 'Under what circumstances would you abandon your criterion of rationality?', Popper should reply, 'When it is falsified'. Lakatos' arguments against the existing methodologies consisted simply of the exhibition of counterexamples. Now, for a Popperian, a single counterexample kills a theory, so by Popperian standards, Lakatos has successfully destroyed all the rival methodologies. By this point in the argument, however, Lakatos is no longer a Popperian philosopher of science. It would be perverse to maintain a Popperian outlook in philosophy, having abandoned it at the level of physical science. Lakatos develops instead the 'methodology of historiographical research programmes', which is, as the name suggests, a historical analogue of his philosophy of science (vol. I, pp. 131–2).

The motivating thought is that *all* intellectual history is written within some philosophical framework. Lakatos expresses this point by rewriting the distinction between 'internal' and 'external' history (cf. vol. I, p. 102). Internal history is usually understood as the history of ideas (who wrote what, when and to whom), while external history is usually taken to be 'social' history (kings, battles, revolutions). Conceived this way, the internal/external distinction carries no philosophical baggage. Lakatos, however, divided historical writing into a normative-rational part and a socio-psychological part. The normative part supplies a rational reconstruction of the growth of objective knowledge. That is, it presents the development of some body of learning in a way which explains why it counts as knowledge. In order to do that, there must be some (possibly implicit) epistemology at work. For example, an inductivist writing the history of physics will attempt to reconstruct the history in such a way that our present theories turn out to be justified on inductivist grounds. The inductivist methodology is called on to explain why this is a history of *knowledge*, and not merely a history of *beliefs*. Another way to put it is that a methodology sorts the past into rational and non-rational episodes. The rational episodes, taken together, constitute a rational reconstruction of the history in question. The other kind of historical writing, the socio-psychological part, is there to take up the slack. Every method-ology represents some historical episodes as non-rational, and these need to be explained by appeal to sociology and psychology. Lakatos labelled the normative-rational part 'internal' history and the socio-psychological part 'external' history.

Clearly, this Lakatosian distinction between internal and external history cuts at different points for different methodolo-gies: episodes which count as rational on inductivist grounds may count as non-rational by conventionalist lights. Hence, a scientific methodology (i.e. a proposed solution to the demarca-tion question) is not just a code of scientific honesty, but is also the 'hard core' of a historiographical research programme. Lakatos claimed that 'all historians of science *who hold that the progress of science is progress in objective knowledge*, use, willy-nilly, some rational reconstruction' (vol. I, p. 192). That is, every history of science has such a hard core, even if it is not acknowl-edged. Further, the internal history is primary, in that the task of external history is to explain causally whatever episodes the internal history fails to reconstruct rationally.

What is on offer, then, is a deeper relationship between history and philosophy. So far, philosophy has been answerable to history. Now, by regarding the various methodologies as histori-ographical research programmes, it is possible to characterise the relationship between history and philosophy in more detail. Historiographical research programmes have to explain and to predict (or rather, 'retrodict') phenomena in the history of science just as scientific research programmes have to illuminate the physical universe. The standards for evaluating a historical research programme are much the same as those for a scientific programme: 'progress in the theory of scientific rationality is marked by discoveries of novel historical facts, by the recon-struction of a growing bulk of value-impregnated history as rational' (vol. I, p. 133).

These two criteria are the historical analogues of empirical and heuristic progress in scientific programmes, respectively. For example, on the 'empirical' side, Popperian historiography predicts that moments of theory-change are marked by great, falsifying 'crucial experiments'. If, armed with this prediction, Popperian historians went to the archives and found it borne out, their theory would have shown 'dramatic' empirical progress over its rivals. For a 'heuristic' example, Popperian historians have a hard time explaining why apparently rational scientists hang on to falsified theories. They might manage to produce some *ad hoc* explanation, or they might claim that the scientists in question are irrational after all. The methodology of scientific research programmes can easily explain the behaviour in question, because it follows straight from the realisation that research programmes supersede each other by attrition, and that there is rarely a unique moment at which a programme dies. That is, Lakatos can explain the 'anomalous' behaviour of scientists hanging on to falsified theories by direct appeal to his 'hard core', without needing to invent any historical 'epicycles' (cf. vol. I, p. 135). His explanation is therefore 'heuristically progressive'. This 'heuristic' requirement on historical research programmes can be summarised as follows: a methodology must agree as far as possible with the settled judgments of the *élite* as to which episodes in the history of science were rational and which not, without recourse to *ad hoc* devices.

One consequence of the analogy between scientific and historical research programmes is that the relationship between philosophical theory and the accumulated value-judgments of the scientific community can be modelled on the relationship between an empirical theory and the relevant evidence. Usually, a scientific theory is answerable to the established body of 'basic statements', but a really progressive research programme can impose changes on that body. Similarly, theories of rationality must by and large respect the mass of value-judgments and theory-evaluations, but a really progressive historical programme will raise questions that have not previously been addressed. It might even overturn some previously settled judgments (cf. vol. I, p. 132). Lakatos' methodology of historiographical research programmes is therefore not simply élitist, because it shows how the judgments of the *élite* can be overruled by a progressive historical programme. His philosophy of science does not simply describe and systematise the 'given' mass of values and practices. Indeed, one might say that for Lakatos, the 'normative given' is just as much a myth as the 'empirical given'. He starts by taking the vast bulk of scientific practice and judgment for granted, but he regards every element of this basic material as defeasible in principle by a sufficiently progressive theory of rationality. A further consequence of the analogy is that he can deal with the claim that every method-ology of science on offer has been falsified.[7] For Lakatos, this is neither a surprise, nor a problem. Every scientific theory is falsi-fied too, but that was a problem for Popper, not for science. Theories of rationality, like scientific theories, 'remain forever submerged in an ocean of anomalies' (vol. I, p. 134). These anomalies do not show that theories of rationality are nonsense any more than experimental anomalies show that physics is all nonsense. For Lakatos, historical anomalies only present a problem to a programme if it has become clear that they can only be absorbed by *ad hoc* means, and even then it is only permissible to abandon a programme if there is a better alternative available. Notice that these standards apply to external history, too.

HACKING'S INTERPRETATION

Ian Hacking (1979) has usefully drawn attention to the impor-tance of Lakatos' Hegelian background ('Imre Lakatos's Philosophy of Science').[8] According to Hacking, Lakatos hailed from a tradition which takes it for granted that 'Kant undid the notion that for a proposition to be true it must represent some-thing else' (p. 385). Kant thought that representational theories of truth always open the door to scepticism, for we can never know that our representations are accurate. Kant required an account of what it is for a proposition to be true upon which he could construct an anti-sceptical epistemology. No representa-tional theory of truth could meet this requirement. In the Central European idiom identified by Hacking, it is simply naive to press on with representational theories of truth after Kant.

On Hacking's reading, Lakatos inherited the problem of supplying 'a theory of objectivity without a representational theory of truth' (ibid., p. 384). In English-speaking philosophy, says Hacking, Lakatos found a commitment to certain attractive values, such as communication, objectivity and adversary discussion, which were, unfortunately, articulated by means of a commitment to knowledge as representation. The problem, then, was to find some surrogate for truth which would preserve these values without regression to pre-Kantian naiveté. The solution had been anticipated by Peirce and Popper: there is an objective substitute for truth to be found in methodology. Hacking claims that Lakatos' central problem was to develop a methodology which would secure objectivity without appeal to a representational notion of truth. One cannot understand Lakatos without recognising that this is his leading problem, and one cannot see that without acknowledging his Hegelian background. This 'Hegelian' interpretation needs arguing, if it is to succeed, because Lakatos himself never set out his project in these terms, and only once gave his work any sort of Hegelian gloss (P&R, pp. 144–6).

The clearest piece of evidence in favour of Hacking's interpretation is the reply Lakatos made to a criticism voiced by Kuhn (amongst others). Kuhn's (1970b) complaint ('Notes on Lakatos', pp. 142–3) is that when Lakatos writes history, he cheerfully fiddles with the evidence so that the narrative in his main text conforms to the methodology of scientific research programmes. The actual history, when it does not conform so well to Lakatos' model, is related in footnotes. Kuhn's claim is that history cannot have any philosophical function if the details are swept out of the way whenever they become inconvenient: 'what Lakatos conceives as history is not history at all but philosophy fabricating examples. . . . When one's historical narrative demands footnotes which point out its fabrications, then the time has come to reconsider one's philosophical position' (ibid., p. 143). We already know part of what Lakatos would say to this: there is no reason to embrace naive falsificationism in history when we reject it in physics. Historiographic research programmes are also born into a sea of anomalies, and it is only rational to abandon one research programme if there is a better one available. Hence Lakatos can consistently stick with his methodology, warts and all, until something better comes along. He says more than this though:

> I hold that all histories of science are *always* philosophies fabricating examples. But, equally, all physics or any kind of empirical assertion (i.e. theory) is 'philosophy fabricating examples'. Surely since Kant and Bergson this is a commonplace. But, of course, some fabrications in history are better than others. And I offer sharp criteria using which one can compare rival fabrications both in physics *and* in its history, and I claim that my fabrications contain more truth than Kuhn's.
>
> (vol. I, p. 192)

Lakatos' exasperation at having to explain philosophical 'commonplaces' to his distinguished colleagues is consistent with Hacking's interpretation. It is, after all, characteristically Hegelian to think that philosophy advances by cancelling out earlier positions. It also helps Hacking that the 'commonplaces' in question are due to Kant and Bergson.

On the other hand, there are passages in which Lakatos worries about the relationship between methodology and truth. Anyone who offers a methodology for science, says Lakatos, must claim that following the given rules will more than likely lead science towards the truth. Otherwise the whole business is pointless:

> Only such an 'inductive principle' can turn science from a mere game into an epistemologically rational exercise; from a set of lighthearted sceptical gambits pursued for intellectual fun into a, more serious, fallibilist venture of approximating the Truth about the Universe.
>
> (vol. I, pp. 113–14)

The only real question is what logical status this principle should have. Lakatos thought that we cannot argue for it without circularity. Therefore, we should simply adopt it because rationalism requires it. Our present purpose is to evaluate Hacking's Hegelian interpretation of Lakatos, and this passage (together with a more extended discussion at vol. I, pp. 159–67) present a serious problem,[9] for Lakatos cannot have regarded methodology as a *substitute for* truth if he was worried about the relationship between these two. Furthermore, throughout these passages Lakatos seems to employ a very un-Hegelian conception of truth. He writes, here at least, as if for him a true theory is one which accurately describes a reality which is as it is quite independently of our efforts to understand it. Reality, in this view, does not depend for its existence on human cognitive activity, nor is it changed by our inquiries.

In view of these passages in which Lakatos seems to assume a straightforward realism, Hacking's Hegelian reading is too neat. Lakatos was not a thoroughgoing Hegelian in disguise, nor is his work on the philosophy of science a crisp synthesis of Hegel and Popper. Rather, what we have is a philosopher who thought of himself as a descendant of Popper but whose work is characterised by piecemeal survivals from his Hegelian-Marxist education. The chief of these is his understanding of the relationship between history and philosophy.

HEGELIAN HISTORY

Foremost among Lakatos' critics was Paul Feyerabend. He objected that the methodology of scientific research programmes is prey to four kinds of arbitrariness: it arbitrarily selects the last 200 years of science as its target for reconstruction; its standards are too weak to exclude anything, so its appraisals turn out to be arbitrary; it selects research programmes arbitrarily; and it actually reconstructs a streamlined image of science, without arguing for the particular streamlining principles employed (for a succinct statement of these objections, see Chapter 10 of Feyerabend's *Philosophical Papers vol. 2: Problems of Empiricism*). Instead of trying to meet these criticisms individually, I shall argue that beneath these accusations of arbitrariness there lies a misconception concerning Lakatos' philosophical method. Feyerabend, it seems, would have Lakatos argue for his appraisals and his selections of programmes and streamlining principles in advance of his rational reconstructions. However, such arguments would have to be made *a priori*. They would be temporally and logically prior to the empirical study. Such apriorism was not open to Lakatos. Instead, Lakatos attempted to write his historical papers in such a way that the narrative itself argues for its own presuppositions.

The use of historical narrative as philosophical argument is part of Lakatos' Hegelian inheritance. For Hegel, history is a bit like a huge Platonic dialogue. Just as a dialogue starts with simple ideas and progresses dialectically towards a sophisticated conception of whatever happens to be under discussion, so the history of humanity begins with simple forms of consciousness and develops towards a perfect final state. Unlike a Platonic dialogue there is no Socratic figure but the unity of the narrative is maintained by the fact that it is a single rational process. Of course, the underlying unity and rationality of history are obscured by a lot of messy detail, and it is the task of philosophy to winnow out the necessary 'world historical' developments from the contingent chaff. The result is not history, but philosophy-through-history. With that in mind, it may be helpful to take some liberties with the minutiae of history in order to clarify the underlying dialectic. Hegel's distinction between *history proper* and *history in the service of philosophy* licenses a little circumspect rewriting of the past, and this is the source of Lakatos' relaxed attitude to Kuhn's accusations of data-rigging.

To see the point, suppose that there really was a discussion of justice in ancient Athens. Suppose it to be like Plato's *Republic*, except that being real live people, the participants were not nearly so well disciplined nor so eloquent as Plato's characters. In particular, Thrasymachus (who considers justice to be that which is advantageous to the strong) arrived late. The debate had been going round in circles because others had been tiptoeing around his position without daring to come out and endorse it. At the same time, other conceptions of justice had been developed and were quite advanced compared with his rather simple contribution. Hence, Thrasymachus' late arrival caused the debate to get bogged down for a while, and distorted its evolution. Now, Plato wants to transcribe this discussion in a way which brings out the logic of its development and exhibits the superiority of the view which emerges at the end. Rather than reproduce the debate word for word, with all its false starts and dead spots, he tidies it up, eliminating a lot of coughs and irrelevant interjections. He has Thrasymachus enter early, thereby placing his remarks at a logical moment in the debate and dispensing with a lot of aimless chat. The result is a less accurate record of the facts, but a clearer account of the argument. This, for Hegel, is the task of philosophy: to lay bare the rational development underlying the details of history.

Some picture of this sort seems to lie behind Lakatos' understanding of the task of philosophy of science. In order to bring out the rationality of the history of science, it may be necessary to tidy up the details a bit. It is only to be expected that the actual history of science should be a muddled affair with blind alleys and aimless meanderings when compared with the underlying rational process, just as our imagined actual Athenian debate is more obscure than Plato's streamlined account. It is because Lakatos was concerned to expose the objective dialectic of the history of science that he endorsed Popper's tripartite ontology. Popper held that the most modern philosophers had mistakenly treated the epistemology of science as a problem about beliefs, that is, a question about the cognitive states of scientists. Popper observed that very little scientific knowledge resides in the consciousness of scientists; no scientist is capable of remembering every detail of his own works, let alone those of his colleagues. Most of our knowledge is stored not in brains, but in libraries. Hence, in addition to the 'first world' of physical stuff, and the 'second world' of mental states, there is for Popper a 'third world' of 'objective contents of thought' (Popper 1972, p. 106). This 'world' contains the contents of books, libraries and journals. It also contains objects which may not have been written down in one piece but could be assembled by 'cutting and pasting' from books and journals, such as theoretical systems, problems, problem situations, critical arguments and conjectures.

Lakatos inherited from Popper the view that the third world is essential if we are to understand what it is for science to be objective:

> The rationally reconstructed, growth of science takes place essentially in the world of ideas, in Plato's and Popper's 'third world', in the world of articulated knowledge which is independent of knowing subjects. . . . Kuhn's research programme seems to aim at a description of *change* in the ('normal') scientific mind (whether individual or communal). But the mirror-image of the third world in the mind of the individual, even in the mind of the 'normal', scientists is usually a caricature of the original; and to describe this caricature without relating it to the third-world original might well result in a caricature of a caricature.
>
> (vol. I, pp. 92–3)

Perhaps no one present at the Athenian debate fully understood the logic of its development except Socrates, but the history of science has no Socrates. We are interested in the argument itself, not the partial versions of it reproduced in the minds of the participants. Nor do we care much about the motives of the speakers. Perhaps Thrasymachus counted himself among the strong, and so had selfish reasons for taking up his view. That psychological explanation, whatever its merits, makes no difference to our understanding of the argument. The 'third world' is necessary, according to Lakatos, if we are to separate the argument itself from the beliefs and desires of the participants in the dialogue; but we must be able to identify the underlying argument if we are to exhibit the rationality of the process. Otherwise there is no way of showing that the final conception to emerge is any improvement on the starting point.

This Hegelian picture of history may explain Lakatos' relaxed attitude to Kuhn's criticism, but it also allows a pointed restatement of Feyerabend's criticisms. Hegel thought that the broad outlines of history are necessary, and necessarily progressive. Hegel was able to map out his dialectic on several levels; the *Phenomenology of Spirit* traces the development of consciousness from the simplest empirical level to a full understanding of Hegel's system; the *Logic* advances from the concept of being by means of a dialectic of categories; and the political history traces the necessary advance towards the rational state. Hence, if Feyerabend's question (Why this tradition?) had been asked of Hegel (i.e. Why does his speculative history of freedom and reason take place mostly in Europe and why does it terminate in Germany?), he could have replied that only the history of Europe displayed the form demanded by the *Logic* and the *Phenomenology*. Whatever else may be said about Hegel's system, it does have the advantage that the necessary form of history is argued for independently of the empirical study of history itself (cf. Taylor 1975, pp. 219–20). It is this metaphysics, together with the formal deduction of his logic, that organises Hegel's reconstruction of history and licenses his progressivism. Lakatos' history has no such metaphysical underpinnings. Instead, Lakatos had to rely on the sheer coherence of his narratives to make the case for his selections of programmes and periods, and his streamlining principles. This may strike philosophers as reckless, but the alternative was a retreat to apriorism.

Lakatos was, above all else, convinced that there must be a rational structure to the history of science, but offered no independent argument for this claim. The reason for this is, I think, as follows. One would only expect to find a methodology displayed in the history of science if one thought that some sciences at least really are getting closer to the truth. For, if there really is progress in science, then this fact stands in need of explanation. Neither sheer luck nor occult flashes of genius are acceptable explanations. Therefore, humanity must have *argued* its way from simple folk beliefs to the scientific theories of the present day. In short, *if* science progresses *then* there must be a coherent thread of argument running through the history of science. The general structure of this argument is what we mean by 'the scientific method'.

The problem, of course, is the 'if'. We may think that our science is nearing the truth because it delivers such effective technology. However, one can make a very loud bang with a bottle of dephlogisticated air, and it is perfectly possible to tell the time with the aid of geocentric astronomy. Moreover, it is possible that our corner of spacetime is untypical, in which case an accurate description of our immediate surroundings will be an inaccurate general theory of the universe. As Hume argued, all our beliefs about the future depend on an unargued assumption that the future will resemble the past in the relevant respects. In other words

> There is no ultimate proof that, even where Elizabethan beliefs were replaced in the course of progressive problemshifts (like beliefs about heat, magnetism), we have been heading towards the Truth. We can only (non-rationally) believe, or, rather hope, that we have been. Unless hope is a 'solution', there is no solution to Hume's problem.
>
> (vol. II, p. 223)

The task of philosophy, therefore, is not to prove that our science is real knowledge of real Reality. Rather, it is to lay out the dialectics of growth, the world-3 development of knowledge; not with a view to convincing ourselves that science does indeed progress (we are already sure of that) nor with the intention of explaining the beliefs and actions of individual characters (that is the task of ordinary history). The point is to understand the growth of knowledge without mystification or dissimulation, that is, without having to posit a rare and mystical faculty of genius or intuition, and without having to maintain the fictions of justificationist epistemology. Charles Taylor summed up Hegel's mission thus:

> Philosophy defends the rationality of the real and purifies it, keeping it from the corruption which would beset it if it were to be generally misunderstood by the various merchants of irrationality, both Romantics and reactionaries.
>
> (Taylor 1975, p. 425)

One need only substitute 'sceptics' for 'Romantics' and 'élitists' for 'reactionaries' to capture the spirit of Lakatos' polemical efforts.

Since Lakatos had no pure dialectic of categories with which to buttress his historical dialectic, he lacked Hegel's conviction that history is necessarily progressive. He argued instead that science progresses *all being well*. Therefore, Lakatos' historical papers had to argue (empirically) for the methodology of scientific research programmes, while at the same time they had to display the methodology at work in whatever episode happened to be in question. The former task requires fidelity to the fine details of history, while the latter does not. It is no wonder that critics found Lakatos to be something of a moving target.

OTHER HEGELIAN TRACES

There is in the methodology of scientific research programmes a Hegelian thought about the explanation of change. For Hegel (1929), change is explained as the resolution of accumulated tension within a complex dynamic unit. 'Contradiction is the root of all movement and life, and it is only in so far as it contains a contradiction that anything moves and has impulse and activity' (*Science of Logic* Bk II, Section I, Chap. II, Part C, Obs. 3).

For something to contain a contradiction does not mean, for Hegel, that it entails both *A* and *not-A* for some proposition *A*. A Hegelian 'contradiction' is better understood as an internal tension. What it means is that the elements of the object grate against each other in some sense appropriate to the kind of object in question. Now, a Lakatosian research programme is a dynamic unit. Its constituent parts interact and modify each other (in particular, the hard core and heuristic combine to act on the 'protective belt'). It may not even be possible to characterise one part of a research programme in isolation from the others. In the jargon, the parts are essentially related. A research programme is in this sense an organic whole. A programme 'contains a contradiction' (in the Hegelian sense) when it becomes unable to protect its hard core without violating the spirit of its positive heuristic. This tension is eventually relieved by a problem-shift to a new programme.[10]

Other Hegelian elements in Lakatos' work include his insistence that an epistemology must meet its own standards. For Hegel, philosophy advances when the standards set by an epistemology for any knowledge are applied to the epistemology itself. This is precisely how Lakatos developed his position from that of Popper. The point of the historiography is to allow the methodology of scientific research programmes to turn on itself. Furthermore, the only universal rule of scientific conduct in Lakatos' methodology is that scientists must keep score honestly. That is, they may stick with degenerating programmes in the hope of a revival, but they must acknowledge the degeneration. In other words, the cardinal intellectual virtue, for Lakatos as for Hegel, is self-consciousness. Finally, there is the backward-looking nature of Lakatos' methodology. Human beings can only appreciate the underlying rationality of scientific practice *after* the event because the rationality in question belongs not to individual scientists but to science itself. In Hegel's image, 'The owl of Minerva spreads its wings only with the falling of the dusk' (cf. Taylor 1975, pp. 423–5).

CONCLUSION

Almost all the serious opposition to the methodology of scientific research programmes comes from historically-oriented philosophers such as Kuhn and Feyerabend. Most of their arguments address the adequacy of the methodology as a reading of the history of science. The ahistorical philosophies of Popper and the positivists are nowhere to be seen, because by the late 1960s there had been a profound problem-shift away from *a priori* investigations of the 'logic of science' in favour of debates about rationality in which historical case studies play an indispensable role. Popper's original demarcation question really had developed into a competition among rival historiographies of science, as Lakatos claimed. (Perhaps Feyerabend's 'anarchism' is too unsystematic to be described as an historiography, but the point stands all the same, because his views on rationality in science take the form of an opinion about the reading of the history of science.)

The credit for this problem-shift in the philosophy of science away from formal logic and towards historical case studies belongs above all to Kuhn. *The Structure of Scientific Revolutions* is primarily an anti-positivist polemic. It was not possible, after the publication of this work, to maintain a conception of scientific rationality which was so completely at variance with scientific practice. The real problem for positivists (and Popperians too) was not Kuhn's large thesis (that there are scientific revolutions as he describes them). The lasting damage was done in the detail. Once philosophers had been exposed to the history of science it was all over for pre-Kuhnian forms of rationalism. Rationalist philosophers who did not wish to abandon the idea of scientific reason had no option but to refine it so as to accommodate the facts of history. The methodology of scientific research programmes was Lakatos' attempted refinement.

Chapter 5

The politics of reason

In evaluating Hacking's 'Hegelian' reading of the methodology of scientific research programmes, we saw that Lakatos considered the proper aim of science to be the truth (rather than, say, technological advancement or increasingly refined puzzle-solving). Moreover, he seemed to assume an uncomplicated view of truth in which a theory is true if it corresponds with reality.

His preference for a correspondence account of what it is for a theory to be true was not merely a consequence of falling among pre-Kantian savages. Lakatos made his motivation clear at the several points where he quotes with approval from Bertrand Russell's (1935) polemic against pragmatism, *The Ancestry of Fascism*.[1] Russell's claim is that once we abandon the representational notion of truth, there is nothing to prevent a despot from defining good method as that which serves the state, or the party. If truth is *that to which we all agree in the end* then there is no basis on which to complain that agreement has been improperly secured. For, how can there be a compelling criterion of 'proper' inquiry if we have no conception of objective truth? Thus, says Russell, pragmatism eventually comes to serve fascism, in spite of the good intentions of the original pragmatist thinkers. *The Ancestry of Fascism* is Russell's version of an argument advanced by many writers in this century. The common theme is a philosophical struggle between virtuous rationalists who employ Reason in pursuit of Truth and wicked irrationalists who deny the reality of Reason and Truth, preferring to celebrate Passion and the Will. This struggle is politically significant, (say the rationalists) because with rationalism goes a respect for freedom, while the natural politics of irrationalism is totalitarianism.

Notable rationalists for our purposes (apart from Russell himself) were Popper (*The Open Society and its Enemies*), Michael Polanyi (*Science, Faith and Society*, Chapter 3), Edmund Husserl (*The Crisis of European Sciences*) and György Lukács (*The Destruction of Reason*), with whom the young Lakatos had some direct contact. A remarkable feature of this argument is that the same philosopher can appear either as a sheep or a goat depending on the version in hand. Hegel, for example, is a rationalist for Lukács but an irrationalist for Popper. Polanyi is an irrationalist in Lakatos' book because of his commitment to the 'tacit dimension' (that is, the intuitive feel a scientist has for his work). Isaiah Berlin contends that Hume was sufficiently irrationalist in his philosophy to lend arguments to the German counter-enlightenment.[2] Nietzsche, of course, is always numbered among the wicked irrationalists. Nevertheless, the argument structure is the same, and Lakatos' polemics against élitist philosophers of science fit smoothly into this tradition (particularly vol. II, Chapters 6 and 11).

Lakatos seems to concur with his fellow rationalists that irrationalist philosophers are almost all decent fellows who unwittingly threaten free civilisation by giving intellectual comfort to tyrants. As Lukács put it:

> A philosophical stance cannot be 'innocent'. Bergson's own philosophy of morality and history did not lead to fascist conclusions. But with regard to his human responsibility, that is totally irrelevant beside the fact that without falsifying his philosophy Mussolini was able to develop a fascist ideology out of it . . . the possibility of a fascist, aggressively reactionary ideology is objectively contained in every philosophical stirring of irrationalism. When, where and how such a, seemingly innocent, possibility turns into a dreadful fascist reality is not decided philosophically. . . . But insight into this connection should heighten the thinking man's sense of responsibility, not blunt it.
>
> (Lukács 1980, p. 32)

Lukács' characterisation of the problem and its solution bears further comparison with Lakatos' work. Here is Lukács again:

> The disparagement of understanding and reason, an uncritical glorification of intuition, an aristocratic epistemology, the

rejection of socio-historical progress, the creating of myths and so on are motives we can find in virtually any irrationalist.

(ibid., p. 10)

This is almost exactly Lakatos' accusation against Kuhn and Polanyi:

All élitists lay great stress on the inarticulable, on the 'tacit dimension' of science. But if the 'tacit dimension' plays a role in normative appraisal, the layman obviously cannot be a judge. For the tacit dimension is shared and understood (*verstanden*) only by the élite. Only they can judge their own work. Thus in this tradition we have a combination of élitism and of a cult of the unarticulated and, indeed, of the inarticulable.

(vol. II, p. 227)[3]

Kuhn is an élitist for Lakatos because only the relevant scientific community is qualified to judge whether a discipline is in crisis or not. Worse still, Kuhn offered no criteria by which the experts could make that judgment. If it feels like a crisis to the élite then it is a crisis, and if not then it is not. Thus (to use Lukács' language) Kuhn glorifies the intuitions of the scientific aristocracy.[4]

LAKATOS' RATIONALISM

Having located Lakatos in the tradition of writers for whom rationalist epistemology is conceptually tied to democratic politics, we now need to ask: what precisely is rationalism for Lakatos?

The central thought is that *reason is the fundamental category in historical explanation*. The precise content of this formula depends in part upon what it is that we hope to explain. As a historian, one might be concerned with the actions of an individual human being, or with some larger scale event such as the English civil war or the scientific revolution. Lakatos was solely concerned with developments in science and mathematics, and had little to say about the deeds of individual people. He was, remember, committed to the view that philosophers should ignore the psychological states of particular scientists (world-2) in favour of the objective development of knowledge (world-3). However, I shall first sketch the outlines of rationalism at the personal level before discussing Lakatos' version of the rationalist thesis. There are three reasons for this. First, rationalism is easier to understand at the personal level. Second, it is at this level that rationalism connects most directly with liberalism. Third, this distinction between the rationality of persons and the rationality of historical processes explains some of the divisions within the rationalist camp.

First then, rationalism at the individual level. In order to understand the speech and behaviour of an individual historical character, one should (if one wishes to be a rationalist) begin with the assumption that this person spoke and acted for reasons. If we could ask 'why did you do that?', then (if the person is not mad) some rational explanation should be forthcoming. Such an answer makes a connection between the speech or deed in question and some goal or value held by the agent. In the most straightforward cases, the action can be shown to be a means to some specifiable end. Thus reasons can also be historical explanations. What it means for reason to be a *fundamental* category is that such reasons are not to be analysed away in favour of some other kind of explanation. Specifically, the reasons that people give are not typically fronts for ulterior motives, nor are human beings helpless conduits for material forces (such as the will-to-power, class interest, unconscious drives, excessive black bile, unpropitious planets, etc.). In short, rationalists prefer explanations of human action that cite reasons rather than material causes.[5]

This distinction between reason-citing explanations and cause-citing explanations is the basis for most rationalist accounts of the human condition. Suppose Peter is blown against Paul by a strong wind. In this case, Peter is merely a link in a causal chain and cannot be held responsible for the consequences. If we asked him 'why did you do that?' he could fairly reply that he did not actively *do* anything. On the other hand, if he deliberately barged into Paul, we can demand a reason. What is more, his answer can be evaluated in ways that a causal explanation cannot. There can be good reasons (perhaps Peter hoped to push Paul out of the path of a falling piano) but not, in this sense, good causes. A strong gust of wind may be a sound explanation but it is not the chosen means to any goal. Notice that Peter's reason can be good in two senses: we can evaluate both the means and the end. In this example, pushing Paul is presumably an effective means of moving him to safety, and saving his life is a morally estimable goal. Thus, on a rationalist account, the distinction between reason-citing explanations and cause-citing explanations is essential if we hope to discriminate between actions for which one can be held responsible and events at which one merely happened to be present.

The above is only a sketch. A rationalist theory of action would have to address problems such as weakness of the will, the origins of goals and preferences, the unconscious and the status of animals. Nevertheless this picture is enough to illustrate the connection between rationalism and liberalism. On a rationalist account the most important fact about any human being is that he or she *acts*. That is, this person chooses means and ends and can be held responsible for those choices. Our choices enjoy a special dignity because, on views of this sort, choosing is essential to our humanity. My choices, and the reasons I give for them, are mine in something like the way that my body is mine, which is to say that they are in part constitutive of me. This claim is mirrored in English idiom: it makes sense to ask 'what are your reasons?' but not 'what are your causes?'. To frustrate the free choices of a rational agent is, for a liberal rationalist, an outrage similar to bodily assault. Therefore the leading political problem is to protect the free choices of individual citizens from interference by other people and, especially, by the state. Thus rationalism is the basis for an argument against illiberal government. A crucial part of this story, indeed one of its attractive features, is that it applies to all rational agents everywhere, regardless of accidents of birth and differences of culture and history. If I meet another human being, I should treat this person with respect and consideration *not* because he belongs to my clan, *nor* because he is a great hunter but simply because he is a rational agent like me.

Something like the above is implicit in Popper's *The Open Society and its Enemies* and may have been part of Lakatos' thinking, though he never committed anything on the subject to paper. Had he done so, he would have found himself engaged with one of the most difficult issues for rationalists: the relationship between rationality in individual people and rationality in historical processes. Popper's line on this question was relatively clear. For Popper, anyone who sees necessity in human history cannot be a true liberal. Popper imagined that historical necessity must be like physical necessity. If there were laws of historical development like laws of physics then it would be possible to predict the future of human history. This, though, would be a denial of human freedom and spontaneity, and, what is worse, an excuse for submission in the face of tyranny. Popper charged Hegel with precisely this offence. In Popper's view Hegel reduces free human beings to the status of mere conduits for world historical forces. The fairness of Popper's reading of Hegel is open to question, but the important point is that there is a serious problem here for anyone who hopes to find rationality in both individuals and in larger units such as institutions and movements.

As noted, Lakatos never discussed the problem of interpreting individual human beings. His concern was to find rationality in the history of science and mathematics. A typical Lakatosian narrative is thus a rational reconstruction of the life of a mathematical or scientific *thought* rather than that of a person (*Proofs and Refutations*, for example, is the story of the Euler formula). In his work, therefore, the rationalist preference for reasons over causes in historical explanation takes the following form: given a historical episode in which one theory is replaced by another, a rationalist will want to argue that the change happened because the successful theory is logically better than its defeated rival. Thus Lakatos does not only set his face against relativism (the claim that there is no objective sense in which one theory can be said to be better than another). He *also* opposes the claim that the objective superiority of one theory over the rest cannot explain why that theory is adopted as scientific orthodoxy. For the sake of a label, we can call this latter view 'materialism'.[6] The materialist argues that the logical merits of a theory are irrelevant to whether it is adopted or rejected by the scientific community, because the rise or fall of a theory is a sociological event to be explained by the prevailing social and political conditions together with the psychological and economic needs of scientists and their sponsors. It is no more than a fortunate coincidence if the winning theory is also the best. Rationalists like Lakatos, on the other hand, insist that when a poor theory is replaced by a better one it is likely that the logical superiority of the new theory brought about the change.

Lakatos did not imagine that every change in scientific orthodoxy is progress. He liked to cite the cases in which theories were adopted under political pressure from totalitarian governments. In these cases he was sure that change was for the worse. Moreover, he did not think that *any* change in the scientific outlook could be proven beyond all doubt to be a step in the direction of the truth. The scientific community is capable of going astray all by itself, without the assistance of a Stalin-figure. He was especially scornful of the view that every episode in the history of science makes some contribution to our inevitable progress towards a flawless knowledge of the world. The classic (Hegelian) version of this idea has it that every historical event is progressive because 'the Cunning of Reason' is able to turn any sort of human activity to its advantage. When he seemed to find this thought in Stephen Toulmin's *Human Understanding*, he asked (rhetorically), 'Does this mean that we *needed* the Dark Ages in order to get from Archimedes to Galileo?' (vol. II, p. 237).[7] Of course, in a rational reconstruction of the history of this or that idea it is the case that every detail makes some contribution to the argument, but it is in just this respect that rational reconstructions differ from their originals. There is barely a word wasted in Plato's rational reconstructions of the conversations of Socrates. No doubt the original debates were shot through with facetious remarks and irrelevant digressions, but these are of no interest to a philosopher hoping to identify the rational content of the discussion. This is the meaning of Lakatos' remark that 'actual history is frequently a caricature of its rational reconstructions' (P&R, p. 84, n. 2).

Thus, Lakatos' rationalism consisted in the conviction that science in good order is guided by reason. By 'reason' he meant neither the ineffable intuitions of the scientific *élite* nor any 'cunning' metaphysical principle that somehow turns everything (even the collapse of European civilisation) into a progressive event. The rationality that guides Lakatosian science is logical method. It is because his rationalism took this form that Lakatos described himself as a 'demarcationist', for his view does require that there be some general logical method that 'demarcates' science proper from pseudo-science (see vol. II, pp. 108–11). (There is, of course, no guarantee that science will follow this guide, nor can it be proved that logical method must inevitably lead to the truth. Lakatos' philosophy is fallibilist at every level.)

Lakatos' demarcationism has the following features. First, it insists that in addition to practical, 'tacit' know-how (such as knowing how to ride a bicycle) there is also propositional knowledge (such as understanding the physical principles that make two-wheeled vehicles possible). Further, this 'knowledge-that' is what science seeks. This is vital because if instead we emphasise the 'tacit dimension' then knowledge-that is obscured by know-how and the realist goal of articulating true propositions is usurped by the pragmatist aim of effective action. When this happens, according to Russell and Lakatos, there is nothing to prevent a despot from claiming that the aim of science is to serve the state (or the party, or the revolution, etc.). This insistence that the essential part of science is the propositions rather than the laboratory skills (for there are no logical relations between skills) leads Lakatos to endorse Popper's (and Frege's) 'world-3', 'the Platonic world of objective spirit, the world of ideas' (vol. II, p. 108). (It is just because Lakatos' rationalism leads to this conclusion that it was natural to label the opposing view 'materialism'.) However, the defining feature of demarcationism is the conviction that 'the products of knowledge can be appraised and compared on the basis of certain *universal* criteria' (vol. II, p. 109). Of course, demarcationists differ amongst themselves as to what these criteria are, but they all agree that there is some universal standard that can be applied to any scientific product. This allows Lakatos to claim for demarcationism 'a democratic respect for the layman':

> The demarcationist lays down *statute law* for rational appraisal which can direct a lay jury in passing judgment. (One does not, for instance, need to be a scientist to understand the conditions under which one theory is more falsifiable than another.)
>
> (vol. II, p. 110)

In other words, reason is a neutral arbitrator between competing theories. Its role is to ensure fair dealing in the marketplace of ideas.

THE LIMITS OF DEMARCATIONISM

We have already seen why Lakatos thought that some form of demarcationism must be true. If the demarcationist project were to collapse, then, to Lakatos' mind, it would be much harder to resist fascism at the philosophical level. It is therefore remarkable that, by Lakatos' own lights, the demarcationist project cannot be successfully carried to completion.

The reason for this is that, in the words of John Stuart Mill, 'No one need flatter himself that he can lay down propositions sufficiently specific to be available for practice, which he may afterwards apply mechanically without any exercise of thought' (*Aphorisms*, 1837). In other words, given any statute of law there will always be hard cases in which the application of the rules requires some judgment (and if we make rules to govern the exercise of such judgment, the same point applies to these rules and so on to an infinite regress). Lakatos knew this: 'Of course, no statute law is either unequivocally interpretable or incorrigible. Both a particular ruling and the law itself can be contested' (vol. II, p. 110).[8]

The point is particularly telling given the details of Lakatos' own contribution to the demarcation question. Recall that, in his theory, a research programme makes heuristic progress if modifications to the protective belt of auxiliary hypotheses are made 'in the spirit' of the guiding heuristic. Deciding whether or not a particular programme meets this criterion is clearly a judgement-call. Precedent is unlikely to provide much help because each research programme has its own characteristic heuristic 'spirit'. Moreover the 'democratic respect for the layman' must be tempered by the thought that the laity are unlikely to be in communion with the spirit of whatever programme is in question. Only those with a feeling for this spirit could hope to judge whether the programme is making heuristic progress. Hence it turns out that Lakatos' demarcationist criterion can only be applied by an *élite* of people in whom the relevant spirit lives.

Thus a particular ruling depends on an inarticulable 'feeling for the spirit' of the heuristic of a research programme. The law as a whole can be contested too, because Lakatos' entire theory rests upon agreed judgments concerning the merits of past scientific programmes. The methodology of scientific research programmes began from the observation that Popper (and every other demarcationist philosopher before Lakatos) was committed to a criterion which condemned just about every great scientific achievement as 'pseudoscience'. Lakatos' aim was to develop a demarcationist criterion which did not suffer this difficulty. But who gets to decide which episodes in the history of science are the great achievements? The experts, of course. For this reason, Lakatos conceded that 'to a very limited extent élitists have a genuine case' (vol. II, p. 112).

We should not imagine that these concessions to élitism are accidental features of the methodology of scientific research programmes which Lakatos might have avoided with a little more care. In *Proofs and Refutations*, at the beginning of his career in the West, Lakatos announced that 'The growth of knowledge cannot be modelled in any given language' (P&R, p. 93). The reason is that growing knowledge calls novel concepts into being. A radically new concept typically comes about through a complex process of argument and criticism. Crucially, different concepts normally result from different patterns of debate. Consequently, even if we were able to study and model every dialectical pattern to have appeared so far, there is no reason to suppose that no new patterns will present themselves in the future.

This claim that 'one cannot describe the growth of knowledge . . . in "exact" terms, one cannot put it into formulae' (vol. II, pp. 136–7) was important to Lakatos because it provided him with a reply to Feyerabend's criticism that rationalism is actually damaging to science. Feyerabend agreed with Lakatos that each new body of scientific work has its own special characteristics, quoting Ernst Mach with approval, 'The schemata of *formal* logic and of *inductive* logic are of little use for the intellectual situations are never exactly the same'.[9] If this is the case then there is no point in trying to establish strict, universal methodological rules. Indeed, rationalist philosophers who try to press such rules on science can only harm the patient they hope to treat. For, Feyerabend claims, it is historically the case that some of the most widely admired episodes in the history of science came about because the scientists involved followed no rules that any rationalist would propose:

> Ideas which today form the very basis of science exist only because there were such things as prejudice, conceit, passion; because these things *opposed reason*; and because they *were permitted to have their way*. We have to conclude, then, that *even within* science reason cannot and should not be allowed to be comprehensive and that it must often be overruled, or eliminated, in favour of other agencies. There is not a single rule

that remains valid under all circumstances, and not a single agency to which appeal can always be made.

(AM, p. 158)

It is important to realise that by 'reason' Feyerabend means the allegedly universal rules for thought and conduct proposed by rationalist philosophers down the centuries. For him, reason (thus understood) and science are two distinct traditions within western culture and the former is a danger to the latter. Feyerabend likes science because it seems anarchic to him, and he likes anarchy. The grand tradition of philosophical rationalism seems to him like a policeman who, having no feeling for anarchy, mistakes it for disorder and slovenliness.

Feyerabend tried to secure his view by using case studies to show that even the most popular and obvious methodological prescriptions would have blocked scientific progress had they been enforced. It is open to question whether he succeeded in this (see for example Newton-Smith 1981, Chapter VI). What matters for our purposes is his claim that 'Even Lakatos' ingenious methodology does not escape this indictment' (AM, p. 158, n. 11). Lakatos' public reply is as follows:

> My methodology of scientific research programmes does not have any such stern code: *it allows people to do their own thing but only as long as they publicly admit what the score is between them and their rivals.* There is freedom ('anarchy' if Feyerabend prefers the word) in creation and over which programme to work on but the products have to be judged. *Appraisal* does not imply *advice.*
>
> (vol. II, p. 110)

The difficulty with this reply is that appraisal is rather pointless unless it is acted on. A scientist who continued to work on a research programme which he believed to be degenerating would have some explaining to do. Appraisal may not strictly entail advice, but it is certainly a heavy hint, and has serious consequences: 'Those who stick to a degenerating programme . . . can do this mostly only in private. Editors of scientific journals should refuse to publish their papers. . . . Research foundations, too, should refuse money' (vol. I, p. 117).

If this point is admitted then Feyerabend's criticism bites. For Lakatos concedes the possibility that a degenerating programme can sometimes be rejuvenated and become part of the most advanced scientific thinking. Thus, he must admit that a case in which a programme was abandoned as a result of a Lakatosian appraisal could turn out to be grist for Feyerabend's mill. It could be that his rationalist methodology had blocked progress by killing off a programme which would otherwise, eventually, have advanced our knowledge.

Lakatos offered a rather more colourful reply to Feyerabend in private. In a letter dating from the summer of 1970, when Feyerabend was writing *Against Method,* Lakatos protested that he was being misinterpreted:

> Your criticisms seem to be reasonable except for your claim that I am the last stronghold of mechanical rationalism which, of course, is utter nonsense. There is absolutely nothing mechanical about my 'rules' . . . if you go on with this mechanical v. dialectical rationalism, pinning me down with that mechanical nonsense I shall cut off your head.[10]

Lakatos saw no contradiction between the methodology of scientific research programmes and his early thought that every complex scientific idea has a characteristic inner logic. To put the point differently, scientific arguments are not wholly formal; the *content* of an argument matters as well as its *form* (the advantage of historical case-studies for philosophers is that they can exhibit the content of an argument as well as its logical form). It is this inner logic that one hopes to capture in a rational reconstruction. Lakatos' rationalism is not mechanical because it recognises and respects the characteristic logic of each research programme. That is what talk of 'the spirit of the heuristic' is about. It is precisely because each scientific idea has a different inner logic that strict general rules cannot be given. And it is the lack of such rules that forces Lakatos to make concessions to élitism.

In the end, then, Lakatos' rationalism amounts to this: when science and mathematics are in good order they are guided by the natural dialectic of whatever ideas are in play. Feyerabend believes something like this too. After all, his complaint is that methodological rules interfere with something, but what could that be if not the inherent logic of the subject matter in view? To put it another way: Feyerabend quotes Einstein's description of scientists as 'unscrupulous opportunists' (AM, p. 10). Of what does such a scientist take opportunistic advantage? The technical issue between Lakatos and Feyerabend is whether scientists need philosophers to lay bare the dialectics of their work by writing rational reconstructions of it. Lakatos thinks that they do because some scientists (especially social and political scientists) refuse to notice when the inner logics of their pet ideas are all played out.

PROOFS AND REFUTATIONS: AN ANARCHIST TRACT

The fact that Lakatos never quite embraced the mechanical rationalism required of a rigorous demarcationist is not surprising when one considers the open-ended and ambiguous discussions of reason in *Proofs and Refutations*. Part of his critique of mathematical formalism is that formalists only recognise two methods: there is the sort of mechanical rule-following that computers can be programmed to do, and there is lawless insight and sheer luck. *Proofs and Refutations* is intended to show that 'this bleak alternative between the rationalism of a machine and the irrationalism of blind guessing does not hold for live mathematics' (p. 4). Indeed, it would be in the spirit of Lakatos' enterprise to observe that mechanical rationalism and irrationalism are a dialectical pair, like justificationism and scepticism. For, once a mechanical rationalist announces that rationality is a matter of following some precisely specified set of universal rules, an irrationalist only has to argue that some apparently rational institution (such as science) does not in fact follow these rules.

In the main text of *Proofs and Refutations* the pupils try to formulate rules to guide their mathematical activities. However, every heuristic method presented in the dialogue is shown to have its limitations. If Alpha's concept-stretching 'method of surrender' had been consistently followed, we should very soon have been left with no informal theorems at all, as Delta observed (P&R, p. 16). On the other hand, if Delta's 'method of monster-barring' had been rigorously obeyed, there would have been no hope of progress, because Delta's method is to legislate against the shifts in meaning necessary for knowledge growth. Similarly, Beta's 'method of exception-barring' is limited in that it is still linguistically conservative, because it recommends the delineation of the 'domain of validity' of the conjecture within the existing taxonomy. Such conceptual innovation as there is under Beta's method can only be a re-ordering of the existing ontology (for example, Beta distinguished convex polyhedra, but the underlying polyhedron-concept was not fundamentally changed). Zeta's 'method of deductive guessing' (P&R, p. 76) eventually degenerates into a chain of trivial generalisations (P&R, pp. 81 and 98).

The 'method of lemma-incorporation' was capable of producing proof-generated concepts, and so overcame this linguistic conservatism (P&R, pp. 89–90). However, the method of lemma-incorporation (and its generalised form, the method of proofs and refutations) leads to infinite regress and 'frustrating logico-linguistic pedantry' (P&R, p. 56). As more lemmas are incorporated in the statement of the theorem, so the definitions become increasingly unwieldy. The work of the proof is transferred to the logical terms and the original extra-logical mathematical content of the theorem eventually plays no role in the proof. However, a purely logical proof can only prove a logical truth: the mathematical content of the theorem is thus disconnnected from the proof (P&R, pp. 102–3). This process may only be resisted if we are confident that the mathematical concepts are sufficiently stable to resist stretching (as may be the case with elementary number theory, for example). Moreover, the trend towards increasingly radical concept-stretching may reach the most fundamental logical terms.

Finally, Lakatos made it clear that in his opinion Epsilon's method, which we might call the 'method of formalisation', also had its limits, and indeed that mathematics was beginning to run up against them. Considered as a principle, Epsilon's method says: express all proofs in formal logic. Like all the preceding methods, this 'method of formalisation' was initially a progressive step. The shifts of meaning associated with Epsilon's 'translation' of the problem into algebraic and logical terms allowed him to produce a single account of ordinary Eulerian polyhedra and Eulerian star-polyhedra (P&R, p. 120). In common with the other methods, however, Epsilon's Euclidean-formalist way of doing mathematics produces a kind of degeneration if pursued exclusively. Hence, Lakatos considers that *all* the heuristic rules canvassed in the dialogue result in degeneration if followed to the bitter end, including Epsilon's principle of only considering proofs given in a purely formal idiom. The élitist Alpha and mechanical-rationalist Gamma despair of the situation:

ALPHA   Lambda's rules for *'rigorous proof-analysis'* deprive mathematics of its beauty, present us with the hairsplitting pedantry of long, clumsy theorems filling dull thick books, and will eventually land us in vicious infinity. Kappa's escape-route is convention, Sigma's mathematical pragmatism. What a choice for a rationalist!

GAMMA   So a rationalist ought to relish Alpha's *'rigorous proofs'*, inarticulate intuition, 'hidden lemmas', derision of the Principle of Retransmission of Falsity, and elimination of refutations? Should mathematics have no relation to criticism and logic?

(P&R, p. 54)

Feyerabend's 'anarchism' lay in the fact that he refused to endorse any methodological rule unconditionally, and in this sense the Lakatos of *Proofs and Refutations* is a methodological anarchist.

We saw earlier that 'anarchism' of this sort requires a concession to élitism. It is therefore not surprising to find a place in *Proofs and Refutations* for mathematical taste. Zeta's method of 'deductive guessing' produced a chain of ever more general formulae. Gamma complained that these generalisations were becoming increasingly trivial – the generalisation to the case of the twin-tetrahedra amounts to little more than a calculation. Clearly, we want to stop the chain of generalisations at the point where increases in scope cease to bring increases in depth. But, 'Who decides *where* to stop? Depth is only a matter of taste' (P&R, p. 98). Gamma offers a solution:

Why not have mathematical critics just as you have literary critics, to develop mathematical taste by public criticism. We may even stem the tide of pretentious trivialities in mathematical literature.

(P&R, p. 98)

to which Lakatos adds the following thought in his own voice:

Quite a few mathematicians cannot distinguish the trivial from the non-trivial. This is especially awkward when a lack of *feeling for relevance* is coupled with the illusion that one can construct a perfectly complete formula that covers all conceivable cases.

(P&R, p. 97, n. 2; italics added)

This 'feeling for relevance' can only be an inarticulate intuition enjoyed by members of the mathematical élite. Thus the difficulty of avoiding mechanical rationalism without giving in to élitism and irrationalism is present from the beginning of Lakatos' serious work on science and mathematics.

REASON AND FREEDOM

It seems, then, that Lakatos was a methodological anarchist of sorts all along. This needed some analysis to establish because on the one hand the Lakatos of *Proofs and Refutations* is quite frank and open about the difficulties for rationalism posed by the history of mathematics; on the other hand, the inventor of the methodology of scientific research programmes usually writes as if demarcationism were the only serious option and all dissenters either knaves or fools. The reason for this is not hard to find: *Proofs and Refutations* is a polemic against formalism, while the theory of research programmes was developed to oppose Kuhnian irrationalism. This is why the meaning-considerations that occupy the final third of *Proofs and Refutations* are almost wholly absent from Lakatos' accounts of problem-shifts in physics (for the exceptions, see vol. I, pp. 25, n. 2, 101, and vol. II, p. 150). Formalist philosophers of mathematics err by overlooking the dialectics of concept-formation, so it is natural for a critique of formalism to stress the point. At the same time, the more rationalism becomes dialectical the less content it seems to have. A rationalism which finds rationality in the specifics of whatever subject matter is in view has relatively little to offer in the way of topic-neutral universal rules.

If the above is true, then what was the deep basis of Lakatos' disagreement with Feyerabend? The difference between them was not merely that Lakatos thought that scientists ought to allow their theories to be appraised by laymen.

Part of Feyerabend's objection to rationalism is that when some set of practices and propositions is judged to be a necessary part of rationality it becomes difficult to criticise them without seeming to embrace irrationality. Suppose (to take a trite example) it is established that a coherent essay identifies a pair of opposing positions and offers five points in favour of each before choosing one over the other. A student who finds not two but three views on some question will stand accused of trying to write several essays at once. Teachers will explain that the *logical* course would be to take the positions in pairs. If the student persists in ignoring the established method she or he may be dismissed as a crank or failed as a dunce. Or as Feyerabend put it,

> A society that is based on a set of well-defined and restrictive rules, so that being human becomes synonymous with obeying those rules, *forces the dissenter into a no-man's-land of no rules at all and thus robs him of his reason and his humanity.*
>
> (AM, p. 162)

Feyerabend goes on to claim that many so-called irrationalists imagine that in order to oppose some particular conception of rationality, they must promote mysticism and absurdity.

The reason why it is difficult to criticise some specific organon is that logical laws have long been regarded as self-evident truths. On this traditional view, anyone who understands the rules of rational thought and action must see that they are binding. Such understanding is, of course, a sign of rationality. Therefore, anyone who does not see the truth of these laws even after they have been explained in detail and at length cannot be fully rational. The point has political consequences, because (it is often argued) it is only rational creatures that can hold rights and responsibilities. Only rational creatures can be admitted to the moral community. Non-rational creatures deserve compassion, not liberty (which is why we have a duty to feed our pets but are not required to respect their choices). If an entire culture fails to recognise rationality as such, then it is evidently not yet capable of self-government.

This point cannot be directed at Lakatos, however, because he did not believe in self-evident truths. For him, formal logic is 'a paradigm of informal, quasi-empirical mathematics just now in rapid growth' (P&R, p. 5). The scope of Lakatos' fallibilism includes formal logic and, indeed, the theory of rationality in general. The sceptic Kappa asks a naive rationalist among the students:

> Can we stretch the concepts in your theory of rationality? Or will that be manifestly true, formulated in unstretchable, exact terms which do not need to be defined? Will your theory of criticism end in a 'retreat to commitment': is everything criticisable except for your theory of criticism, your 'metatheory'?
>
> (P&R, p. 104)

It is logically impossible for a thoroughgoing fallibilist to erect uncriticisable rational norms. Here again then, Lakatos and Feyerabend are in agreement.

The divide comes over the relationship between science and rationality. For Lakatos, modern science is paradigmatically rational and the natural place for a theorist of rationality to seek a model. Consequently, although he can criticise individual scientific programmes, Lakatos cannot offer any critique of science as a whole. For Feyerabend, science is just one epistemological tradition among many. It is open to him, therefore, to bring extra-scientific standards to bear on scientific practice. However, Feyerabend cannot offer a general critique of science because he does not regard science as a sufficiently unified entity (the rationalist tradition in philosophy, on the other hand, is coherent enough to merit analysis and appraisal). This difference can in turn be traced to a political question: what is the greatest present danger?

Like many Eastern European émigrés, Lakatos thought that the most serious threat to freedom comes from the state. A state in the grip of a totalitarian ideology assumes the right (and grants its police the powers) to interfere in every corner of public and private life. Everything from fine art and international sport to agriculture and human fertility is bent to the service of the ideology. Science can resist this kind of intellectual and social monoculture because it has its own objective methods and goals. If scientists stick to the rational pursuit of truth then at least one human activity can be saved. However, ideologists in power have all manner of persuasive means for bringing science into the service of the régime. It is therefore vital to articulate the goals and methods of science with all the clarity possible. Furthermore, if philosophers could establish non-partisan standards for criticising and judging theories and ideologies, then it would be possible to evaluate the prevailing state ideology (and, almost certainly, find it wanting). Lakatos believed in a theory-neutral universal rationality because, looking at the contest between Nazi anthropology and ordinary 'scientific' anthropology, he felt there must be some non-question-begging grounds for ruling in favour of the latter. It was natural to describe the situation by saying that the Nazis were breaking the rules of good scientific practice. It is then a task for philosophers to work out what those rules are.

For Feyerabend totalitarian government is a problem but not *the* problem. For him the really serious problem is the hegemony of the western scientific outlook. The distinguishing mark of a totalitarian ideology is that it recognises nothing of value outside itself. For True Believers it is beyond criticism, for a critic must occupy some standpoint of his own, but there is no objective standpoint outside the big theory. It is a truism that ideologies are most effective when they work without the aid of state police, show-trials and the rest of the usual totalitarian apparatus. The most successful ideologies are freely accepted by people who regard them not as defeasible theories but as manifest facts (as in 'we hold these truths to be self-evident'). Now, most propagandists for the scientific method fit this description precisely. For Feyerabend, scientific rationality is not an ideologically neutral magistrate for the marketplace of ideas. Rather, it is one of the competing ideologies. Like all the best True Believers, scientific rationalists do not recognise the possibility of criticism from outside their system. For, how could there be any objective basis for disputing the excellence and objectivity of the scientific method? Thus for Feyerabend the cult of the scientific method has all the characteristics of a totalitarian ideology and produces equally damaging results. The moral impetus behind his work is the damage that has been done to non-western cultures by the imposition of 'rational' and 'scientific' agriculture, medicine and government. Thus the most pressing task is to expose scientific (or better, scientis*tic*) rationalism for the totalising ideology that it is. (Which is not to say that Feyerabend is against science. On the contrary, science is one of the native cultures he hopes to protect against scientistic rationalism.)

Feyerabend's view is not without its problems. At the academic level, his reading of the history of science does not command universal assent. Politically, his freewheeling approach to non-western traditions faces the difficulty that western science and rationalism are not the only dangerous ideologies. Some cultures (including our own) considered witchcraft to be a capital offence; others held that the continuing existence of the universe depends on human sacrifice; the tiger and the rhinoceros face extinction because parts of their bodies are used in Chinese medicine. It is easy to plead for tolerance towards relatively harmless traditions such as astrology and mysticism. Feyerabend is usually silent on the more gruesome alternative technologies. A demarcationist can appeal to his model of the scientific method to argue that the theories underlying these practices are false (or poorly supported by the evidence, or extremely degenerate, etc.). It is not obvious how Feyerabend could make a case for stopping witch-burning, human sacrifices and tiger-poaching. Indeed, it is arguable that Feyerabend's relaxed attitude is only possible because the triumph of the west has greatly reduced these and other horrors. Finally, he suffers the usual problem of naive liberals: what to do when faced with an ideology which does not accept liberal standards. The normal solution is to tolerate anything except denial of the rules of civilised, rational debate on the grounds that these rules are theory-neutral and therefore to insist on them is not to prejudice any substantive issue one way or the other. Having rejected this option, it is not clear what else is open to him. It is not therefore surprising that he failed to mention the Rushdie affair in his 1992 preface to the third edition of *Against Method* in spite of his long-standing interest in the relations between cultures.

Suppose that, on these grounds, we decide that there must be something right about rationalism. There must be non-question-begging grounds for arguing that certain dangerous practices are unnecessary because the relevant beliefs are false. What can Lakatos offer us in this direction?

The first thing to observe is that fallibilism, if taken seriously, prevents the swaggering arrogance of which Feyerabend complains. No sincere fallibilist could march into an ancient agri-cultural community and insist that the people give up their established methods in favour of some untested scheme. However, this virtue comes at a cost, because fallibilism makes it impossible to oppose anything absolutely. For example, in the long-running controversy over the teaching of evolutionary theory in American schools, no fallibilist can claim that evolu-tionary theory is established fact while creationism is conclusively disproved. Lakatos will say that evolution is a progressive research programme while creationism is degener-ating, but his account allows for the possibility that creationism will eventually rediscover progressive power and win out on logical grounds. It is possible for fallibilists to argue that some theories are so much better supported than others that there is no real contest.[11] However, when the judge asks whether evolution is a theory or a body of established fact, an honest fallibilist must answer that it is a theory. It would not be surprising if, on the basis of this advice, the judge ruled that evolution and creation should both be taught since they are both theories (even if one is at present very much better supported than the other).

The second lesson is that we cannot establish a theory of rationality in the abstract, without reference to anything else. There must be plenty of background agreement concerning both empirical facts and evaluative judgments. It is possible for creationists and evolutionists to have a reasoned (if rather bellicose) exchange because they agree that there is such a thing as objective science and that Newton, Galileo, and Einstein were great scientists. The question is: which biology is properly scientific? Creationists quote Popper to claim that evolution is not really science; evolutionists reply that if *that* is what you mean by science then Newton was no scientist; and so on. Creationists, and Marxists, set out to show that their views meet the highest standards of scientific rigour. This claim to scientific good standing opens such doctrines to criticism by science-based theories of rationality, such as the methodology of scientific research programmes. Even allowing for the claim that demarcationism is strictly speaking false, it is possible to assemble a loose list of methodological desiderata. However fiercely they fight over the fine details, demarcationists are remarkably united about the sorts of features they like to see in a scientific theory. This consensus is enough to defeat at least the crudest pretenders to scientific status. (On this point, Lakatos and Feyerabend differ, because Lakatos could easily subscribe to a weakened demarcationism which only hoped to record general scientific values, while Feyerabend sees no point in even this modest exercise.)

The sort of close-quarters struggle within 'western' culture exemplified by the 'monkey trial' is one thing. The standoff between American anthropologists and religious fundamentalists in the Native American tradition, who reject 'white science' in its entirety, is quite another. Here there is no agreed common ground nor any neutral method to mediate between rival substantive claims. If there were a set of self-evident norms governing all disputations then there should be at least that much common ground. But there is not.

Third, demarcationists must ensure that their topic-neutral rules fit the historical record. However, the act of elaborating a methodology to accommodate the endless variety of logical patterns in the history of science has the effect of draining out its content, until we are left with a methodology that forbids almost nothing. If at this point we wish to remain rationalists, it must be a dialectical rationalism that insists that there is a specific logic to each subject matter. This rationalism, however, cannot be relied on to do the political work that demarcationists normally require. For suppose that some subtle charlatan were to defend a bogus theory by exploiting the weaknesses of demarcationism. Strictly speaking, the most that we can complain of is that he has failed to follow the natural dialectic of whatever question is in view. But then we are left with a clash of subjective (if expert) intuitions about the naturalness of this or that theoretical development. This is not enough to foil a determined zealot.

Chapter 6

After Lakatos

The methodology of scientific research programmes has attracted many admirers but few followers. The fate of *Proofs and Refutations* is still more paradoxical. Widely praised, it has enjoyed very little serious scholarly attention. This is perhaps because, unlike the methodology of scientific research programmes or Kuhn's scientific revolutions, *Proofs and Refutations* does not offer a simple logical scheme for philosophers to apply more or less mechanically to the history of any given discipline. *Proofs and Refutations* is, perhaps, too complex and ambiguous to be the first of a genre. The aim of this chapter is to suggest some reasons for the reception of Lakatos' work and to speculate a little regarding future developments.

DIAGNOSIS

Lakatos' problems with the methodology of scientific research programmes began when he tried to apply it to new cases. He had a particular difficulty with the Copernican revolution. It would have been especially embarrassing if the triumph of Copernican theory had turned out to be irrational by the standards of Lakatos' methodology. The development of heliocentric astronomy was not only the (arguable) foundation of the scientific revolution. It was also one of Polanyi's leading examples of the 'tacit dimension' of scientific work. According to Polanyi, good scientists can tell by intuition which theories will turn out the best even before the evidence is in and the experiments conducted. He says,

This is indeed the kind of foreknowledge the Copernicans

must have meant to affirm when they passionately main-tained, against heavy pressure, during one hundred and forty years before Newton proved the point, that the heliocentric theory was not merely a convenient way of computing the paths of planets, but was really true.[1]

Kuhn, the other leading 'élitist' in Lakatos' demonology, had produced a book-length study of the episode.[2] The core of the argument in Feyerabend's *Against Method* is a tendentious recon-struction of Galileo's part in the rise of heliocentric astronomy. The Copernican revolution is a severe test for any theory of scientific change.

Lakatos was satisfied with his account of what it is for a programme to progress, as described in Chapter 4, until he realised that it is not able to explain the *early* success of Copernican astronomy (vol. I, p. 184). Recall that empirical progress is the successful prediction of 'novel facts, facts which had been either undreamt of, or have indeed been contradicted by previous or rival programmes' (vol. I, p. 5). The Copernican heliocentric cosmology predicted that the apparent positions of the stars should vary through the year as the earth moves round its orbit. This effect was not properly detected until the 1830s, but heliocentric cosmology had effectively replaced the geocen-tric tradition by the middle of the seventeenth century. The Copernican system also predicted the phases of Venus, but these were not observed until 1616, *after* the theory began to gain currency.[3] The lack of empirical evidence in favour of the helio-centric view before that date was compounded by serious empirical problems. Any theory which had the earth moving seemed to predict constant high winds, and Copernicus had to explain why people were not thrown off the spinning planet by centrifugal force. Rationalist theorists of scientific change have to show that the Copernican revolution was rational in its early stages in spite of these and other problems.

In a joint paper of 1973 (with Elie Zahar), Lakatos carefully identified a 'Pythagorean–Platonic research programme' (vol. I, pp. 180–4) and argued that both the Ptolemaic and Copernican systems are part of it. In this analysis, the Ptolemaic system is a degeneration of that programme since the Platonic heuristic requires the paths of heavenly bodies to be uniform and circular, and this rule is violated by Ptolemy. However, it is not enough to show that the Ptolemaic system was sick. By his own standards, Lakatos had to show that the Copernican system was progressive, otherwise the revolution would be a great leap sideways at best. However, his analysis gave him an extra problem. According to Lakatos, the 'Platonic' research programme (in its Copernican form) was 'not further developed but rather abandoned by Kepler, Galileo and Newton' (vol. I, p. 184) in favour of the new 'dynamics-oriented' physics. Hence, if the Copernican programme was not progressive by the early seventeenth century then it was never progressive at all because soon after it ceased to exist. For this reason, Lakatos thought, the observation of the phases of Venus came too late in the day (1616) to explain the success of the Copernican programme (though not too late to explain the success of heliocentric models more generally). Now, Lakatos' theory required a programme to predict novel facts if it was to count as empirically progressive. So it seems that, by the standards of the methodology of scientific research programmes, the Copernican system was not empirically progressive until 1616, whereupon it was abandoned! Something had gone wrong.

In the same paper, Lakatos endorsed a modification to his theory due to Zahar, as follows. A programme can make empirical progress if already known facts which played no part in the emergence of the programme turn out to be ready consequences of the hard core. For example, it is an immediate consequence of the heliocentric thesis that planetary motions display stations and retrogressions when viewed from the Earth. It does not matter that Copernicus had to make complex *ad hoc* adjustments to the details of his theory in order to render it observationally adequate. In that respect he was no better off than the Ptolemaic astronomers. The point is that the central idea of his theory explained why there should be planetary stations and retrogressions *at all*, whereas the Ptolemaic theorists could only cope with these phenomena by *ad hoc* parameter adjustment (vol. I, p. 185). Similarly, it follows from the basic model that 'if an astronomer takes the Earth as the origin of his fixed frame, he will ascribe to each planet a complex motion one of whose components is the motion of the sun' (vol. I, p. 186). Crucially, Copernicus could predict these and other structural astronomical phenomena before making any observations. This explanatory power, according to Lakatos, made the Copernican theory superior to the Ptolemaic version from the very beginning.

Zahar's idea is plausible, though it is hard to state as an objective logical principle. The most natural formulation is to say that a programme is empirically progressive if it predicts some known fact for which it was never intended to provide an account. The difficulty is that the evaluation of programmes is supposed to be a world-3 exercise, so the intentions of the theorist should be irrelevant. However, the significance of this episode for the present purpose lies elsewhere.[4] The case of the Copernican revolution showed that the task of characterising progress and degeneration in research programmes is open-ended. That is, there might always be some illustrious scientific success story which is not progressive by Lakatos' standards. Lakatos would then have to expand his definition of progress accordingly, just as he did when confronted with the Copernican revolution.[5] The paper on Copernicus marks the beginning of a degenerative phase for the programmes programme, because from then on its modifications were data-driven. Lakatos insisted that a progressive programme can pretty well ignore the facts so long as it shows theoretical progress and can supply some evidence that the outstanding anomalies will disappear as the programme becomes more sophisticated under the guidance of its heuristic. Degenerating programmes are characterised by *ad hoc* rearguard actions to deal with recalcitrant evidence. Hence Lakatos' theory is, ironically, able to explain its own decline.

It might be argued that Zahar's innovation need not signal degeneration in the programmes programme because it led to new discoveries in the history of science.[6] On this view, empirical progress is far more important than heuristic progress and so it does not really matter if Zahar's innovation did not grow naturally out of Lakatos' philosophical heuristic. There are two difficulties with this train of thought. One is that what goes for the Copernican revolution goes for any scientific success story. Suppose that it is necessary to tack on lots of new criteria as more and more of the history of science falls under Lakatosian analysis. If this process were iterated sufficiently the methodology of scientific research programmes would become indistinguishable from the methodological casuistry that demarcationists so abhor. This point stands even if *all* of the new criteria lead to empirical progress in the history of science. The second difficulty is that Lakatos did not choose the word 'programme' lightly. The requirement of heuristic progress is intended to mark the difference between a dynamic intellectual system and an unstructured collection of disparate ideas. To admit just any empirically progressive addition is to rob the programmes programme of its systematicity.

Historians of the philosophy of science may feel that the above account is too neat and tidy. A complex historical event is not to be explained by a single logical point, however subtly ironic and reflexive. This objection is a good one, and reminds us of Kuhn's remark that Lakatos' history 'is not history at all but philosophy fabricating examples' (quoted at vol. I, p. 192). Lakatos' reply was to reiterate his theory of history and its rational reconstructions. This may have alienated philosophers and historians alike. Let us, therefore, consider some other possibilities besides the above 'internalist' account.

Historians, who tend to take a dim view of philosophical storytelling anyway,[7] are unlikely to appreciate the suggestion that 'The very *problems* of the historian are determined by his methodology (i.e. theory of appraisal)' (vol. I, p. 190). This makes it sound as if one cannot be an historian without being a philosopher first. It is then hardly surprising if historians suspect an attack on the autonomy of their discipline. It is true, of course, that an historian's work is conditioned by his background commitments. All arguments, including historical ones, have premises. However, Lakatos wrote as if each historian of science should have one clear theory of knowledge, and each historical event should have one explanation. In fact, historians (unless they are in the grip of some totalising ideology) practise a subtle eclecticism. It is quite normal for an historian to explain a single event on several levels at once and to admit several different kinds of explanation into the same account. Indeed, skill in weaving many explanatory strands into a single narrative rope is part of an historian's professional competence. Hence, historians can fairly complain that Lakatos did not understand the logic of their activities (this may be a remnant from his Marxist days; Marxists tend to imagine that all history-writing is irredeemably partisan).

Quite how far Lakatos can be said to have misunderstood the nature of historical knowledge depends, of course, on one's theory of history. In the view of the historian G.R. Elton, history is distinguished by 'its concern with events, its concern with change, its concern with the particular' (Elton 1969, p. 21). Demarcationist philosophy of science might, at a pinch, claim some interest in events and in change. However, the chief goal was always the establishment of a general logic of science rather than the historical understanding of particular episodes. Elton's view of history as the study of particulars for their own sakes is not unchallenged in the literature. Another historian, E.H. Carr, argues the importance of generalisations in historical thinking. However, even he warns us not to 'suppose that generalization permits us to construct some vast scheme of history into which specific events must be fitted' (Carr 1990, pp. 64–5). The logical schemes proposed by demarcationist philosophy of science are not normally 'vast', but they are rigid and hence they interfere with the historian's efforts to understand the specifics of past events. That criticism applies to the methodology of scientific research programmes even though Lakatos' scheme is more flexible and context-sensitive than most.

Part of the problem is that Lakatos hoped to use the same method of appraisal for historical research programmes as for scientific research programmes. This sins against the view of those like Collingwood who see an essential difference in logic between historical explanations and explanations in the physical sciences:

> In the organization of meteorology, the ulterior value of what has been observed about one cyclone is conditioned by its relation to what has been observed about other cyclones. In the organization of history, the ulterior value of what is known about the Hundred Years War is conditioned, not by its relation to what is known about other wars, but by its relation to what is known about other things that people did in the Middle Ages.
>
> (*The Idea of History*, p. 250)

If Collingwood is right, then the instinct of an historian is to set the Copernican revolution in its correct intellectual and social context. To try to work it up into a general theory of scientific revolutions is as unhistorical as to try to fit the Hundred Years' War into a general theory of wars.

The ambition of philosophy to establish a universal model of scientific argument is compounded in historians' eyes by the wilful one-sidedness of philosophical narratives. Hegel hoped to extract a purely rational, dialectical process from the sound and fury of human history, and made it clear that this effort was a different enterprise from the writing of history proper. Demarcationist philosophers make a virtue of excluding psychological and social considerations from their accounts of science. This is the point of Lakatos' reinterpretation of the split between internal and external history. He may have abandoned the crude distinction between the contexts of discovery and justification, but his refusal to admit personal and social elements into his reconstructions has the same effect. For a historian it is shockingly arbitrary to decide in advance that a certain sort of evidence shall not be considered. Some historical questions (Why did that happen *then*? Why this person and not some other?) cannot normally be answered without reference to personal and social facts. Elton, considering the assistance that an historian can provide to colleagues in neighbouring disciplines, claims that,

> He can help them to understand the importance of multiplicity where they look for single-purpose schemes, to grasp the interrelations which their specialization tends to overlook, to remember that the units in which they deal are human beings.
>
> (Elton 1969, p. 55)

Elton had in mind social scientists rather than philosophers of science. Nevertheless his remark goes some way towards explaining the general antipathy of historians of science to theorists of methodology, of which Lakatos is not the only victim. It is open to philosophers to argue (with Hegel) that they are engaged in a different sort of writing from historians, though in doing so they may relinquish any claim on historians' attention.

Let us turn now from historians to philosophers. Philosophers may have begun to realise that in order to accept Lakatos' system, it is necessary to adopt an appropriate account of what philosophy is. Lakatos' practice suggests that for him the chief task of philosophy is to extract the rationality from history, to burnish it and to present it in a pure form. This conception of the discipline has a long history, but it is unlikely to be popular with scientifically-minded philosophers in the English-speaking tradition. Lakatos' invocation of Kant and Bergson cannot have helped here either. Hacking's Hegelian reading of Lakatos may be too neat, but it points in the right direction. Philosophy has spent much of the twentieth century coming to terms with the great systems of the past, of which the most comprehensive and influential is that of Hegel. English-speaking philosophy drew on its empiricist traditions and rejected Hegel and his successors outright. The story of the Moore-Russell revolt is a founding myth of analytic philosophy. The contemptuous dismissal of metaphysics by the Vienna circle positivists is similarly celebrated. Philosophers in the continental traditions have, on the whole, adopted less radical attitudes to the great dead system-builders. Indeed, it is still normal for continental philosophers to define their theoretical perspectives through commentary on and contrast with the intellectual monuments of synthetic philosophy. The widespread conviction in the English-speaking philosophical world that there is little of any value in these works seems dogmatic and implausible to continental philosophers. In this sense, Lakatos was a continental philosopher because for him the question 'What shall we do with Hegel?' was a live one.[8]

More serious than his unfashionable Marxist-Hegelian beginnings was the fact that Lakatos inherited some opponents from Popper. In particular, other realist/rationalist philosophers argued as follows: as realists, we agree with Lakatos (and Popper) that the aim of science is truth (as opposed to saving the appearances, better technology, etc.). As rationalists, we expect means to be properly connected with ends. Specifically, we expect scientific methodology to be connected with the aim of science, that is, the truth. In Lakatos there is no logical or causal connection between his proposed methodology and the agreed aim of increased verisimilitude. All he offers is his metaphysical-inductive principle supported not by argument but by pious hope.[9] Philosophers who argue in this vein hold that the generalised problem of induction is soluble and that a respectable philosophy of science should offer a solution. Clearly, Lakatos' work fails this test. This failure is compounded by the suspicion that Lakatos, for all his demarcationist rhetoric, is too close to Kuhn and Feyerabend in the details of his model.

It is worth noting too that the methodology of scientific research programmes was part of the later stages of a long-lived movement stretching back to the first stirrings of Vienna-circle positivism. Philosophers in the Popperian and positivist traditions had been forced to examine the history of science by Kuhn's *The Structure of Scientific Revolutions* (1962). A decade of historico-philosophical research demonstrated that no single logical pattern was adequate to capture the whole of the history of science. The research programmes model is sometimes useful for talking about theory-change provided it is not imposed too rigidly, but then so are the Kuhnian model, the Hegelian triad and any number of other general logics. Indeed, a glance at the history of such constructions suggests that we should have expected this conclusion. Those models that retain any plausibility do so because they can stretch around the details of whatever case is in hand.[10] Moreover, it is often difficult to say what in a programme is the heuristic and what the hard core. Lakatos had the advantage that it was his theory, so his stipulations were in part contextual definitions. His followers, lacking this advantage, found it difficult to distinguish hard cores from heuristics without leaving a suspicion of arbitrariness.[11] Even Lakatos eventually admitted that 'The demarcation between "hard core" and "heuristics" is frequently a matter of convention' (vol. I, p. 181, n. 1). It is easy to see how it might sometimes be a matter of mere grammar. 'Events of type X have causes of type Y', being an indicative sentence, looks like a candidate for the hard core of some programme. 'In explaining X-events, seek Y-events' is an imperative and therefore part of the heuristic. This confession makes it impossible to present the methodology of scientific research programmes as the beacon of clarity dreamed of by demarcationists.

The connection between politics and the philosophy of science has changed since the 1960s too. Memories of Hitler and Stalin have faded and other concerns have taken the place of the old political imperatives. Environmental anxieties and post-colonial nation-building seem to many to present far more pressing problems than the ever-present danger of totalitarianism that worried Lakatos. Those philosophers concerned with green issues tend to regard science as part of the problem rather than simply as a source of solutions. Theorists of post-colonial politics often share Feyerabend's view that western science and technology (or their apostles, at least) bear some responsibility for the difficulties encountered by the developing world. Consequently, the political motivation behind Lakatos' demarcationism is less widely shared than perhaps it was. Philosophers and historians of science who, for these or other reasons, attach little importance to demarcationism may feel that all Lakatos offers is a more or less Kuhnian picture with a demarcationist gloss. This is hardly surprising since the point of the programmes programme was to combine Popper's demarcationism with Kuhn's historical acumen. This being the case (if one is not motivated to adopt demarcationism) one may as well stick with Kuhn. Moreover, Kuhn (on an aggressively relativistic reading, at least) holds out the promise that physical science can be explained from the perspectives of sociology and cultural studies. Thus Kuhn enjoys the dubious benefit of a large constituency in the humanities for which Lakatos has nothing to offer and towards which he was unambiguously hostile.

Finally, there is a demand for a general critique of science which Lakatos cannot meet because he is, as it were, looking at science from the inside. He develops his normative standards by taking illustrious episodes in the history of science as paradigms of good practice. This being the case, he is not in a position to say anything critical about science as a whole.

PRESCRIPTION

For all of these reasons (and no doubt some others), demarcationism in general and the programmes programme in particular are out of fashion. This is not to say that the efforts of Lakatos and other demarcationists were without value. Like a forest, science seems homogeneous, even monolithic, when viewed from a distance but becomes heterogeneous and complex when examined from close to. Historians have shown philosophers enough detail to demonstrate that any general 'logic of science' is at best a panoramic impression. Still, the view from a distance has its merits. There will always be questions which are not best appreciated with one's nose hard against the bark of some particular tree. The creationism issue in America, for example, or methodological debates in psychology and sociology, or the claims of fringe medicine, all call for some broad sense of what it is to be scientific. The work of demarcationist philosophers of science has enormously improved our ability to compare the logical workings of aspirant sciences (economics, creationism, etc.) with those of the paradigmatic empirical sciences (such as

orthodox physics and chemistry). These comparisons can be illu-
minating even though it is impossible to distil from them a
context-neutral 'scientific method'.

That said, there does not seem to be any future in trying to
revive the methodology of scientific research programmes as a
form of demarcationism. If we hope to develop and to extend
Lakatos' work, the most promising strategy is *not* to turn *Proofs
and Refutations* into a methodology of mathematical research
programmes (as some have tried).[12] It is, rather, to read Lakatos'
essays on the empirical sciences as works of dialectical criticism
like *Proofs and Refutations*. I claimed in Chapter 1 that 'For
Lakatos, philosophy is not the contemplation of eternal verities
but is, rather, an effort to interpret the present in the light of the
past with a view to shaping the future'. What I had in mind were
the passages in *Proofs and Refutations* in which Lakatos argues for
reforms in mathematical practice. In the second appendix ('The
deductivist versus the heuristic approach') he claims that
formalist philosophy of mathematics has a corresponding style
of mathematical practice which he calls the 'deductivist'
approach. This, he claims, is pernicious because it risks permit-
ting mathematics to degenerate into a lot of formally valid
trivialities. Fortunately, his rational reconstruction of the
previous two centuries of mathematical methodology suggests a
reform.[13] This is what I mean by calling *Proofs and Refutations* a
work of dialectical criticism. A rational reconstruction of the
(relatively) recent past can illuminate the present situation in a
way that identifies deep-rooted problems and (one hopes) inti-
mates some remedial action.

The proposal, then, is to read all of Lakatos' work this way.
This may seem to conflict with Lakatos' own understanding of
his philosophy of science. Did he not tell us repeatedly that he
aimed to identify *universal* criteria for the appraisal of scientific
work? Indeed he did, but this ambition stemmed not from his
philosophical curiosity about science, but rather from his
Popperian conviction that demarcationism must be made to
work for the political reasons adduced in the previous chapter. In
Proofs and Refutations, which is free from this political imperative,
he remarks that

> Rationalists doubt that there are methodological discoveries at
> all. They think that method is unchanging, eternal. Indeed

methodological discoverers are very badly treated. Before their method is accepted it is treated like a cranky theory; after, it is treated as a trivial commonplace.

(P&R, p. 136, n. 2)

For 'rationalists' here I think it is safe to read 'demarcationists'. The author of *Proofs and Refutations* understood that methods change in science and mathematics and can be expected to go on changing.[14] The important thing is to try to ensure that such methodological changes are for the better. We cannot leave it to the Cunning of Reason to keep our science and mathematics on track. However, we can only take charge of our own intellectual products if we understand the logic of their genesis. The natural way to do that is by writing a narrative that pays attention to the dialectics of whatever field of study is in view.

Thus, if we abandon the idea that the philosophy of science has to save us from fascism, we can also drop the requirement for universal criteria of theory-appraisal. Indeed, this suggests a general strategy. In developing what Lakatos left us, we should retain just those elements of his thought that are motivated by philosophical curiosity about mathematics and science. Those elements that seem to owe their presence solely to Lakatos' political anxieties can be discarded. Freed of the political baggage, a Lakatosian can face head on Hacking's worry that 'Lakatos has, like the Greeks, made the eternal verities depend on a mere episode in the history of human knowledge'.[15] We can reply that *our* Lakatos (that is, the Lakatos currently under construction) was never hunting eternal verities in the first place. *Our* Lakatos only hoped to understand the dialectic of the last few hundred years of scientific thought. This proposed Lakatos is not obliged to produce one model which captures every scrap of successful scientific thought from Copernicus to the present day. This Lakatos *expects* scientific progress to look different in different centuries just as the author of *Proofs and Refutations* showed that mathematical progress follows different patterns as methodological knowledge develops.

This reinterpretation is licensed by the fact that one cannot accept Lakatos' philosophy as it stands. The contradiction at its core between the demarcationist pursuit of the One True Method and the dialectical sensitivity to changing methods cannot be smoothed away. Forced to choose between politically-motivated demarcationism and philosophically-motivated dialectics, I choose the latter. I also think that this revision does less violence to the actual, historical Lakatos than Hacking's reading.

The dialectical Lakatos of *Proofs and Refutations* faces the problem that it is more difficult for him to fend off relativists, materialists and other irrationalists. This Lakatos must claim that the rationality of mathematics and science lies not in some set of topic-neutral rules but rather in the subject matter itself. This claim cannot be proven, it can only be made plausible by writing up the history in a way that makes this lawless rationality explicit. Materialists (for example) can counter this strategy by offering their own narratives in which the content of scientific and mathematical work is explained causally. That this question should come to a contest of narratives is hardly surprising. We know now that there are very few knockout victories in science or philosophy.

Lakatos is sometimes compared with the later Wittgenstein.[16] The ground for this comparison is Wittgenstein's view that in creating mathematical proofs and in following rules we make choices which affect the evolution of concepts. However, these choices appear in his work as brute facts rather than as rational decisions open to critical evaluation. Consequently, Wittgenstein and Lakatos had quite different conceptions of what philosophy is and what are the interesting questions. Our new improved Lakatos, freed as he is from Popperian prejudices, is a close intellectual cousin not of Wittgenstein but of continental philosophers such as Jean Cavaillès, Gaston Bachelard, Georges Canguilhem and Michel Foucault. Lest anyone suppose that French philosophy is uniformly post-modern and irrationalist, here is Canguilhem on Kuhn:

> For [Kuhn], a paradigm is the result of a choice by its users. Normal science is defined by the practice in a given period of a group of specialists in a university research setting. Instead of concepts of philosophical critique, we are dealing with mere social psychology. This accounts for the embarrassment evident in the appendix to the second edition of the *Structure of Scientific Revolutions* when it comes to answering the question of how the truth of a theory is to be understood.[17]

This question ('How can Kuhn talk about truth?') was for a while the rallying cry of realist-rationalist philosophers of science.

Even Foucault begins to look less radical when he is placed in the French tradition of rationalist, historically-minded philosophy of science from which he sprang.

Lakatos is cousin rather than brother to these French philosophers because there are elements in his work that they would reject. The demarcationism of the methodology of scientific research programmes depends on the supposition that there is an eternal scientific method, which the French school denies. They also oppose any attempt to model the logic of historical research on that of scientific work. However, these objections are not a problem if we are resolved to abandon the rigid, demarcationist spirit of the methodology of scientific research programmes in favour of the more dialectical and historically-minded Lakatos of *Proofs and Refutations*. A more serious barrier to a complete rapprochement is Lakatos' refusal to consider material or technological influences on the growth of scientific and mathematical knowledge. Canguilhem holds that the growth of knowledge normally requires that some extra-scientific conditions be satisfied: 'Quêtelet, for example, studied data about human size; the collection of such data presupposes a certain type of institution, namely, a national army whose ranks are to be filled by conscription'.[18]

For Lakatos these considerations would be banished to irrational 'external' history, for fear of sullying the pure rationality of the 'internal' history of world-3 theories. However, Canguilhem (like Lakatos) thinks that there is a difference between the history of *knowledge* and the history of some or other body of esoteric technical literature, and he further agrees that epistemology has a role to play in making the distinction. He is also adamant that theories and concepts have a privileged position in the history of science, even though he does not subject them to the purdah of internalist history.

> There are always documents to be classified, instruments and techniques to be described, methods and questions to be interpreted, and concepts to be analyzed and criticized. Only the last of these tasks confers the dignity of history of science upon the others. . . . The history of science is interested in, say, the history of instruments or of academies only insofar as they are related . . . to theories.[19]

It is this feature of his view that allows Canguilhem to join Lakatos in the rationalist camp against Kuhn. Thus, *entente cordiale* is possible between Lakatos and the French school, even though doctrinal and methodological differences remain.

The most relevant figure in this group is the philosopher and historian of mathematics, Jean Cavaillès. Cavaillès maintained that mathematics has no need to seek a foundation in anything outside itself. Rather, mathematics is self-generating. It 'weaves itself' using 'threads of necessity'. In other words, Cavaillès saw the possibility of (to use Popper's phrase) epistemology without a knowing subject. Like Lakatos, Cavaillès was interested in the growth of mathematical knowledge. He investigated axiomatic systems, but not because axiomatisation offers an epistemological foundation. His interest lay in the dialectical opportunities presented by axiomatisation. Indeed, he differs from Lakatos in that in *Proofs and Refutations* the development of new concepts and the growth of mathematical knowledge are driven solely by logical operations: conjecture, proof, refutation. A new object enters the system by being either an instance of some conjecture or a (possibly heuristic) counterexample. Formalists (according to Lakatos) mistake the fossilised skeleton of mathematics (i.e. fully formal systems) for the living, growing creature itself. We should not commit the converse error of supposing that living mathematics can prosper without the 'skeleton' provided by the sort of static rationality that formal logic hopes to model. Cavaillès, for his part, holds that non-inferential operations such as abstraction can play a role in the growth of mathematical knowledge. This allows him to consider heuristic ideas characteristic of modern mathematics, including the postulation of new entities to achieve completeness under a given operation (for example, the introduction of complex numbers ensures completeness under the extraction of roots).[20]

Above all Cavaillès shares with Lakatos the relatively rare feature that his philosophical curiosity about mathematics is not swamped by some extraneous philosophical purpose. The philosophy of mathematics currently suffers from an excess of works which hope to show that mathematics poses no obstacle to whatever grand philosophical project is in question. Thus, this writer wants to show that mathematics is compatible with empiricism; that one seeks a place for mathematics within a naturalised epistemology; someone else hopes to demonstrate that everything, including mathematics, can be accounted for by sociology.[21] These works are not necessarily misguided, but it cannot be healthy for the philosophy of mathematics to be dominated by them. It would be false to suggest that Lakatos or Cavaillès is wholly free from anterior philosophical motives, but the historical approach ensures that real mathematics is never far from centre stage.

The point here is not to foist on Lakatos the detailed views of any other philosopher. It is, rather, that these French philosophers spent their careers bringing the benefits of a continental philosophical education to bear on the history of science. Lakatos is therefore a natural member of this group. The lasting value of his contribution to philosophy will only be known when it has been compared in detail with that of writers in similar traditions. It would be ironic indeed if this most pugnacious of philosophers contributed in the end to a reconciliation between the Francophone and Anglophone traditions in the history and philosophy of science. Ironic, but entirely within the spirit of a philosopher who was passionate to the point of belligerence in the defence of reason and objectivity.

Notes

1 LIFE AND CHARACTER

1 Much of the detail here is drawn from a letter from Gábor Vajda to Michael Hallett (Archive, 11.2).

2 'The Jewish Question in Hungary: a Historical Retrospective' in *The Holocaust in Hungary, Forty Years Later*, p. 26.

3 Ian Hacking (ed.) (1981) *Scientific Revolutions* 'Notes on the Contributors'.

2 *PROOFS AND REFUTATIONS*

1 Editorial notes occur on pp. 53, 56, 68, 76, 100, 112, 125–6, 127, 129, 130, 138, 146.

2 Lakatos Archive folder, 12.1, item 12.

3 E.g. D.A. Anapolitanos 'Proofs and Refutations: A Reassessment' in Gavroglu, Goudaroulis and Nicolacopoulos (eds) (1989) *Imre Lakatos and Theories of Scientific Change*. The subtitle to the 1976 volume *Proofs and Refutations: the Logic of Mathematical Discovery* echoes Popper's *Logic of Scientific Discovery*, so it is not surprising if some see *Proofs and Refutations* as an effort to do for mathematics what Popper claimed to have done for natural science. Since Popper thought that there *is* a single, universal pattern of scientific thought, it is a natural mistake to read a similar doctrine into *Proofs and Refutations*, especially in view of Lakatos' later work in which he seemed to take up Popper's quest for *the* scientific method. In this connection it is worth noting that the misleading subtitle was added by Worrall and Zahar, presumably to distinguish the 1976 book from the articles of 1963–4.

4 It is necessary to quote from the thesis here because nowhere in the published version of *Proofs and Refutations* does Lakatos make this point explicitly. His complaint that formalism condemns us to a 'bleak alternative between the rationalism of a [Turing] machine and the irrationalism of blind guessing' (p. 4) and his criticism of 'rationalist' historians of mathematics (p. 134) come close.

5 Lakatos did not write on the later work of Wittgenstein at any length, although he was aware of it and had views on it (see vol. II, Chapter 11). Nevertheless, there is in this criticism of logical positivism a problem for philosophers such as David Bloor who hope to combine *Proofs and Refutations* with Wittgenstein's social account of meaning (e.g. in *Knowledge and Social Imagery* (1976)). Wittgenstein held that confusion and (worse still) philosophy arise when concepts are allowed to stray away from their proper uses. It is important, therefore, to ensure that concepts are kept in their places. The problem is that Wittgenstein offered no way of distinguishing between using a concept incorrectly, and developing a concept in the course of an inquiry. Consequently, the danger of erecting a conceptual prison is as acute for Wittgensteinians as for logical positivists.

Bloor can object that this is a one-sided view of Wittgenstein. In *Remarks on the Foundations of Mathematics* we find the thoughts that proofs play a role in the development of mathematical concepts and that the huge success of mathematical logic obscures important features of mathematics. Moreover, these notes are full of practical examples of concept-stretching. However, Wittgenstein never worked out a stable position on mathematics, whereas the conservative strain in his thinking is part of his developed views on language. More significantly, there is nothing in Wittgenstein to suggest that the choices we make in developing mathematical concepts (and in following rules generally) have any sort of rationality about them. Decisions of this sort appear in his work as brute facts. In a typical piece of tendentious historical argument, Lakatos claimed that 'With the help of a decision-procedure one can decide mechanically whether a conjecture is true or false. Primitive men worship algorithms. Their concept of rationality, like that of Leibniz, of Wittgenstein and of modern formalists, is essentially algorithmic' (vol. II, p. 72). In a word, Wittgenstein is undialectical.

6 See for example Carl Hempel 'Explanation in Science and History', Chapter 1 of Colodny (ed.) (1964) *Frontiers of Science and Philosophy*, London: George Allen & Unwin. Reprinted in *Conceptions of Inquiry*, Brown, Fauvel and Finnegan (eds) (1981) London: Open University Press.

7 By Antoine Goulem.

8 PhD thesis, p. 5, reprinted in vol. II, p. 70 n*.

9 *Physics, Logic and History*, p. 222, Breck and Yourgrau (eds) (1970) New York: Plenum.

Aufheben is a Hegelian technical term. Michael Inwood (1992) discerns three senses: (1) 'to raise, to hold, to lift up'; (2) 'to annul, abolish, destroy, cancel, suspend'; (3) 'to keep, save, preserve' (*A Hegel Dictionary*, p. 283). All three senses are in play in Hegel's usage. In the Hegelian dialectical three-step, the rational part of the thesis is preserved while some erroneous feature is removed and discarded. Thus the thesis is 'raised' to the level of the synthesis. In the absence of a direct English counterpart many translators use the unnatural Latinism 'sublation'. Etymologically the English word most closely related to *Aufheben* is probably 'upheaval', but this is scarcely less misleading.

10 See also vol. II, p. 58.

11 Lakatos is not alone in his criticism of deductivism. V.I. Arnol'd (1992) claims that the development of catastrophe theory was hindered by 'the dominance of the axiomatic-algebraic style', amongst other things (*Catastrophe Theory*, p. 17).

12 As, for example, seventeenth-century results in the theory of equations could not be expressed in the dominant theory of the day, which was geometry. Girard's formulation of the relation between the coefficients and roots of polynomials was beyond reasonable doubt, yet could not be expressed (let alone proved) geometrically. Problems of this sort undermine a dominant theory as effectively as any internal refutation. There is no reason to suppose that all future mathematics will be expressible within that part of logic for which the necessary informal meta-theorems hold. See Larvor (1994) 'History, Methodology and Early Algebra' in *International Studies in the Philosophy of Science* vol. 8, no. 2.

13 In 1641 Evangelista Torricelli constructed a solid of infinite length with a finite volume, and proved the result using the method of indivisibles. He argues, in effect, that the method of indivisibles must be a reliable means of proof because it is such an effective means of discovery (Mancosu and Vailati 1991, p. 52). Or as Kappa put it, 'Discovery always supersedes justification' (P&R, p. 42).

14 Donald Gillies (ed.) (1992) *Revolutions in Mathematics*, Oxford: Clarendon Press.

3 THE POPPER–KUHN DEBATE

1 Margaret Masterman claimed to distinguish 'not less than' twenty-one different senses of 'paradigm' in Kuhn's work (Lakatos and Musgrave 1970, p. 61). See the postscript to the second edition of *The Structure of Scientific Revolutions* (1969) for Kuhn's efforts to disambiguate the term.

2 See Wittgenstein (1958) *Philosophical Investigations*, p. 194.

4 PHILOSOPHY OF SCIENCE

1 Popper had a short Marxist period in his youth. See *Unended Quest*, pp. 31–4.

2 Lakatos was not the first to make this point: see *Structure of Scientific Revolutions*, p. 146; or Polanyi (1964) *Science, Faith and Society*, p. 31: 'In my laboratory I find the laws of nature formally contradicted at every hour, but I explain this away by the assumption of experimental error . . . for if every anomaly observed in my

laboratory were taken at its face value, research would instantly degenerate into a wild-goose chase after imaginary fundamental novelties'.

3 See vol. I, pp. 93–101 for Lakatos on the 'Duhem-Quine Thesis'.

4 Here again, the point had already been made by Kuhn (*Structure of Scientific Revolutions*, p. 154) and Polanyi (*Science, Faith and Society*, p. 23).

5 See Polanyi, *Science, Faith and Society*, p. 92: 'Certain observations may be recognised as establishing formal contradictions to a theory and yet be set aside for the time being'.

6 See Kuhn, 'once it has achieved the status of paradigm, a scientific theory is declared invalid only if an alternate candidate is available to take its place' (Kuhn, *Structure of Scientific Revolutions*, p. 77).

7 For example Feyerabend *Against Method*, p. 249, 'all methodologies, even the most obvious ones, have their limits'.

8 Page numbers refer to the original version of this review, in *Brit. J. Phil. Sci.* 30 (1979), pp. 381–402.

9 I am indebted to W.H. Newton-Smith (1981) *The Rationality of Science*, p. 100, for this point.

10 Recall that Lakatos preferred programmes to theories because programmes can undergo development, while theories cannot.

5 THE POLITICS OF REASON

1 Vol. II, pp. 118–19, 228, 257.

2 'Hume and the sources of German Anti-Rationalism'. Thus the present contrast between rationalism and *irrationalism* is connected historically with the older contrast between the rationalism (or 'intellectualism') of Descartes, Leibniz and Spinoza and empiricism of Locke, Berkeley and Hume.

3 For Polanyi's expression of the 'tacit dimension' see *Science, Faith and Society*, e.g. p. 14, 'The rules of scientific enquiry leave their own application wide open, to be decided by the scientist's judgment'. Polanyi's original motivation was the same as that of Popper: to protect science from interference by totalitarian governments.

4 See, for example, vol. II, p. 111.

5 Metaphysical questions concerning the numerical identity of causes with reasons are irrelevant here. What matters is the distinction between kinds of explanation. Donald Davidson thinks that reasons *are* causes; nevertheless he puts rationality (in the form of the principle of charity) at the heart of his account of human action.

6 This label suggests itself because the view in question is usually motivated by an intuition that abstract objects (such as valid arguments or evidential relations) do not really exist and hence cannot play an essential role in any genuinely explanatory history.

7 Notice that the point would have less rhetorical force if 'Dark Ages' were replaced by 'Golden Age of Islamic Learning'.

8 See also vol. I, p. 117, n. 4.
9 *Erkenntnis und Irrium*, quoted in *Against Method*, p. 10, n. 5.
10 Lakatos Archive folder, 12.8, item 172. The letter is part of a long correspondence during the writing of *Against Method* in which Lakatos and Feyerabend struggle at times to keep their positions distinct. *Against Method* was originally intended to include a reply by Lakatos.
11 See, for example, Philip Kitcher (1982) 'The Case Against Creationism' in his *Abusing Science*, Cambridge, MA: MIT Press, pp. 30–62, 205–8.

6 AFTER LAKATOS

1 M. Polanyi (1966) *The Tacit Dimension*, p. 23, London: Routledge & Kegan Paul, quoted at vol. I, p. 176. In Lakatos' personal copy, this passage is enclosed in a box drawn in green ink.
2 S.T. Kuhn (1957) *The Copernican Revolution*, Chicago University Press.
3 Copernicus died in 1543, and his masterwork (*On the Revolutions of the Celestial Spheres*) was published shortly thereafter. A sketch of his theory was published in his life time, and the theory attracted supporters (including Kepler and Galileo) long before 1616.
4 The thought that a theory is only supported by evidence which was not used in its construction can be detached from the methodology of scientific research programmes and developed independently (cf. Worrall 'Scientific Discovery and Theory-confirmation' in J.C. Pitt (ed.) (1985) *Change and Progress in Modern Science*, Dordrecht: Reidel). It is an open question what degree of exactitude can be achieved in its expression. In particular, there is room for argument as to whether this thought can be formalised mathematically. See D.G. Mayo (1991) 'Novel Evidence and Severe Tests', *Philosophy of Science* 58, pp. 523–52; or J. Earman (1992) *Bayes or Bust? A Critical Examination of Bayesian Confirmation Theory*, pp. 113–35, Cambridge, MA: MIT Press.
5 I should record my suspicion that Lakatos found Zahar's idea independently attractive and seized the chance to build it into his theory. The ground for this suspicion is that he could have dealt with the Copernican revolution simply by taking the entire family of heliocentric models to be a single research programme.
6 And in fact it has been so argued (in conversation) by Francesco Guala. He maintains that my entire presentation of the methodology of scientific research programmes lays too much emphasis on heuristic progress at the expense of empirical progress. He admits, however, that he may be influenced in his judgment by certain philosophers who seem to regard the doctrine of novel facts as the most valuable part of Lakatos' theory. In the philosophy of the physical sciences, this may be true.
7 See Larry Laudan's essay in the Routledge *Companion to the History*

of Modern Science (1990) for a despairing account of relations between the two disciplines.

8 'Since Hegel each generation has unfortunately needed, and has fortunately had, philosophers to break Hegel's spell on young thinkers who so frequently fall into the trap of "impressive and all-explanatory theories [like Hegel's or Freud's] which act upon weak minds like revelations" (cf. Popper, *Conjectures and Refutations*, p. 39). Moore was the liberator in Cambridge before the first war, Popper in the London School of Economics after the second' (vol. I, p. 139, n. 1).

What is significant here is the implicit claim that Hegel alone is responsible for the popularity of over-powered theories. By contrast, Kant thought that it is in the nature of the human mind to seek universal explanations (but then Kant had no need of a philosophical scapegoat for the barbarities of the cold war). It may be true that each generation of *continental* philosophers has to struggle free from Hegel's stifling embrace, but Anglophone philosophers are educated through a different set of texts altogether.

Ironically, Popper spent his later years trying to amplify evolutionary theory into an all-encompassing system of his own (see his *Objective Knowledge*).

9 See, for example, W.H. Newton-Smith (1981) *The Rationality of Science*, pp. 97–9. Lakatos could retort that the fundamental human aims (normally, the true, the good and the beautiful) are unknown in advance of our quests for them. One cannot find out what the good life for a human is *in detail*, without living out some portion of a life. Since we do not know much about these basic ends in advance of our efforts to achieve them, it is pointless to demand that we should have, from the outset, a means to their achievement which can be shown to work (cf. Carr's *What is History?*, p. 119). In the case of knowledge (which I take to be a fundamental aim) this means that we cannot know what a good methodology is until we know a little about what the world is like. In a magical universe full of spirits and purpose, it may well be that seances or ghost-dances are methodologically sound.

10 I once attempted to write Kuhnian-paradigmatic and Lakatosian-programmatic accounts of a crucial period in the development of algebra, in order to see which offered the more plausible account of theory-change in mathematics. As it turned out there was little to choose between them (see B. Larvor (1994) 'History, Methodology and Early Algebra', *International Studies in the Philosophy of Science* vol. 8, no. 2).

11 See C. Howson (ed.) (1976) *Method and Appraisal in the Physical Sciences*. Some of the contributors to this collection of Lakatosian case-studies use the machinery of hard cores and heuristics more systematically, or mechanically, than others. Those papers which borrow their literary structure from the methodology of scientific

research programmes do not, on the whole, read as well as those that take their shapes from the particular episodes in hand.

12 For example, M. Hallett (1979) 'Towards a Theory of Mathematical Research Programmes' (in two parts), *British Journal for the Philosophy of Science* 30, pp. 1–25, 135–59; T. Koetsier (1991) *Lakatos' Philosophy of Mathematics: A Historical Approach (Studies in the History and Philosophy of Mathematics vol. 3)*, Amsterdam: North Holland.

13 This matter is discussed briefly in Chapter 2 of the present work.

14 Lakatos' proposed book on the philosophy of science (which he never managed to start) was provisionally titled *The Changing Logic of Scientific Discovery*. What we cannot tell is whether, in this work, he planned to return to the *Proofs and Refutations* view that *any* methodological precept is open to revision.

15 Ian Hacking (1979) 'Imre Lakatos's Philosophy of Science', *British Journal for the Philosophy of Science* 30, p. 402. Extracts reprinted in Hacking (ed.) (1981) *Scientific Revolutions*.

16 See, for example, Ian Hacking (1979) 'Imre Lakatos's Philosophy of Science', *British Journal for the Philosophy of Science* 30, p. 391. Extracts reprinted in Hacking (ed.) (1981) *Scientific Revolutions*.

17 *A Vital Rationalist: Selected Writings from Georges Canguilhem*, p. 46.

18 *A Vital Rationalist: Selected Writings from Georges Canguilhem*, p. 29.

19 *A Vital Rationalist: Selected Writings from Georges Canguilhem*, p. 30.

20 See Paul Cortois (1996) 'The structure of mathematical experience according to Jean Cavaillès', *Philosophia Mathematica* (3) vol. 4, pp. 18–41.

21 W.D. Hart, in his introduction to the recent Oxford Readings collection on the philosophy of mathematics, seems to think that the most important problem is to avoid Platonism. For a sociological account, see David Bloor (1978) 'Polyhedra and the abominations of Leviticus' and other works. For book-length examples of extraneously-motivated philosophy of mathematics see H. Field (1980) *Science without Numbers* and P. Maddy (1990) *Realism in Mathematics*. The claim is not that Field or Maddy is ignorant of mathematics (plainly they are not) nor that their works are mistaken or pernicious. It is just that the problems they hope to solve (the defence of nominalism and naturalised epistemology respectively) are not specific to mathematics. It is as if the philosophy of history were dominated by wholly general questions about scepticism or materialism.

Michael Dummett (1977), reviewing *Proofs and Refutations*, notes that it 'unlike most writings on the philosophy of mathematics, succeeds in making excellent use of detailed observations about mathematics as it is actually practiced' (*Nature* vol. 267, May). Dummett did not, in that review at least, ask what it is about Lakatos' philosophical approach that makes for that success.

Bibliography

Arnol'd, Vladimir I. (1992) *Catastrophe Theory* (3rd edn) (tr. G.S. Wassermann), Berlin: Springer Verlag.

Berlin, Isaiah (1981) 'Hume and the Sources of German Anti–Rationalism', *Against the Current: Essays in the History of Ideas*, Oxford: Oxford University Press.

Bloor, David (1976) *Knowledge and Social Imagery*, London: Routledge & Kegan Paul.

—— (1978) 'Polyhedra and the abominations of Leviticus', *British Journal for the History of Science* vol. 11, no. 39.

—— (1981) 'Hamilton and Peacock on the essence of algebra', in H.J.M. Bos and I. Schneider (eds) *Social History of Nineteenth Century Mathematics*, Boston: Birkhäuser.

—— (1983) *Wittgenstein: a Social Theory of Knowledge*, London: Macmillan.

Braham, R.L. and Vago, B. (eds) (1985) *The Holocaust in Hungary, Forty Years Later*, New York: Colombia University Press.

Breck, A.D. and Yourgrau, W. (eds) (1970) *Physics, Logic and History*, New York: Plenum.

Brown, S., Fauvel, J. and Finnegan, R. (eds) (1981) *Conceptions of Inquiry*, London: Open University Press.

Canguilhem, Georges (1994) *A Vital Rationalist: Selected Writings from Georges Canguilhem* (tr. A. Goldhammer) F. Delaporte (ed.), New York: Zone Books.

Cantor, G.N., Christie, J.R.R., Hodge, M.J.S. and Olby, R.C. (eds) (1990) *Companion to the History of Modern Science*, London: Routledge.

Carr, E.H. (1990) *What is History?* (2nd edn), Harmondsworth: Penguin.

Collingwood, R.G. (1994) *The Idea of History*, Oxford: Oxford University Press.

Colodny, R.G. (ed.) (1964) *Frontiers of Science and Philosophy*, London: George Allen & Unwin.

Cortois, Paul (1996) 'The structure of mathematical experience according to Jean Cavaillès', *Philosophia Mathematica* (3), vol. 4, pp. 18–41.

Davis, Philip J. and Hersh, Reuben (1982) *The Mathematical Experience*, Brighton: Harvester Press.

Derrida, Jacques (1978) *Edmund Husserl's Origin of Geometry: An Introduction* (tr. J.P. Leavey), New York: Nicolas Hays.

Dummett, Michael (1977) 'Review of *Proofs and Refutations*', Nature, vol. 267, May.

Earman, John (1992) *Bayes or Bust? A Critical Examination of Bayesian Confirmation Theory*, Cambridge, MA: MIT Press.

Elton, G.R. (1969) *The Practice of History*, London: Fontana.

Feyerabend, Paul (1975) 'Imre Lakatos', *British Journal for the Philosophy of Science* 26, pp. 1–18.

—— (1981) *Philosophical Papers Volume 2: Problems of Empiricism*, Cambridge: Cambridge University Press.

—— (1993) *Against Method* (3rd edn) (1st edn 1975), London: Verso.

Field, Hartry (1980) *Science without Numbers*, Oxford: Blackwell.

Gavroglu, K., Goudaroulis, Y. and Nicolacopoulos, P. (eds) (1989) *Imre Lakatos and Theories of Scientific Change*, Dordrecht: Kluwer Academic Publishers.

Gillies, Donald (ed.) (1992) *Revolutions in Mathematics*, Oxford: Clarendon Press.

Giorello, Giulio (1980) 'Intuition and Rigor: Some Problems of a "logic of discovery" in Mathematics' in Maria Luisa Dalla Chiara (ed.) *Italian Studies in the Philosophy of Science*, Dordrecht: D. Reidel Publishing Co.

Hacking, Ian (1979) 'Imre Lakatos's Philosophy of Science', *British Journal for the Philosophy of Science* 30, pp. 381–410 (extracts reprinted in I. Hacking (ed.) (1981) *Scientific Revolutions*, Oxford: Oxford University Press).

—— (ed.) (1981) *Scientific Revolutions*, Oxford: Oxford University Press.

Hallett, Michael (1979) 'Towards a Theory of Mathematical Research Programmes' (in two parts), *British Journal for the Philosophy of Science* 30, pp. 1–25, 135–59.

Hart, W.D. (ed.) (1996) *The Philosophy of Mathematics*, Oxford: Oxford University Press.

Hegel, G.W.F. (1929) *Science of Logic* (tr. W.H. Johnston and L.G. Struthers), London: George Allen & Unwin (first published in German 1812).

—— (1977) *Phenomenology of Spirit* (tr. A.V. Miller), Oxford: Clarendon Press (first published in German 1807).

—— (1985) *Introduction to the Lectures on the History of Philosophy* (tr. A.V. Miller and T.M. Knox), Oxford: Clarendon Press (first published in German 1833).

Hoensch, Jürgen K. (1988) *A History of Modern Hungary 1867–1986* (tr. K. Traynor), London: Longman.

Howson, Colin (ed.) (1976) *Method and Appraisal in the Physical Sciences*, Cambridge: Cambridge University Press.

Husserl, Edmund (1970) *The Crisis of European Sciences and Transcendental Phenomenology* (tr. D. Carr), Evanston: Northwestern University Press (originally published in German 1954).

Inwood, Michael (1992) *A Hegel Dictionary*, Oxford: Blackwell.
Kadvany, John (1989) 'A Mathematical *Bildungsroman'*, *History and Theory* 28, pp. 25–42.
Kitcher, Philip (1982) *Abusing Science*, Cambridge, MA: MIT Press.
—— (1984) *The Nature of Mathematical Knowledge*, Oxford: Oxford University Press.
Koetsier, Teun (1991) *Lakatos' Philosophy of Mathematics: A Historical Approach (Studies in the History and Philosophy of Mathematics vol. 3)*, Amsterdam: North Holland.
Kuhn, Thomas S. (1957) *The Copernican Revolution*, Cambridge, MA: Chicago University Press.
—— (1970a) *The Structure of Scientific Revolutions* (2nd edn), Chicago: University of Chicago Press (1st edn 1962).
—— (1970b) 'Notes on Lakatos', *Boston Studies in the Philosophy of Science* VIII, pp. 137–46.
—— (1977) *The Essential Tension: Selected Studies in Scientific Tradition and Change*, Chicago: University of Chicago Press.
Lakatos, Imre (1961) *Essays in the Logic of Mathematical Discovery*, PhD thesis, Cambridge.
—— (1962) 'Infinite regress and foundations of mathematics', *Aristotelian Society Supplementary Volume* 36 (reprinted in *Philosophical Papers Volume 2*).
—— (1963–4) *Proofs and Refutations*, in four parts in *British Journal for the Philosophy of Science*, 14.
—— (1971) 'History of science and its rational reconstructions' in R.C. Buck and R.S. Cohen (eds) *Boston Studies in the Philosophy of Science 8* (reprinted in *Philosophical Papers volume 1*).
—— (1976) *Proofs and Refutations*, J. Worrall and E. Zahar (eds), Cambridge: Cambridge University Press (consisting of the *BJPS* article plus additional material from the PhD thesis).
—— (1978) *Philosophical Papers* (vols 1 and 2) J. Worrall and G. Currie (eds), Cambridge: Cambridge University Press.
Lakatos, Imre and Musgrave, A.E. (eds) (1970) *Criticism and the Growth of Knowledge*, Cambridge: Cambridge University Press.
Larvor, B. (1994) 'History, Methodology and Early Algebra', *International Studies in the Philosophy of Science* vol. 8, no. 2.
—— (1997) 'Lakatos as Historian of Mathematics', *Philosophia Mathematica* vol. 5, no. 1.
Lukács, György (1980) *The Destruction of Reason* (tr. Peter Palmer), London: Merlin Press (original German edition 1962).
Mach, Ernst (1980) *Erkenntnis und Irrium*, Darmstadt: Neudruck, Wissenschaftliche Buchgesellschaft.
Maddy, Penelope (1990) *Realism in Mathematics*, Oxford: Clarendon Press.
Mancosu, Paolo and Vailati, Ezio (1991) 'Torricelli's Infinitely Long Solid and Its Philosophical Reception in the Seventeenth Century', *ISIS* 82, pp. 50–70.

Mayo, Deborah G. (1991) 'Novel Evidence and Severe Tests', *Philosophy of Science* 58, pp. 523–52.

Newton-Smith, W.H. (1981) *The Rationality of Science*, London: Routledge.

Polanyi, Michael (1964) *Science, Faith and Society*, Chicago: University of Chicago Press.

—— (1966) *The Tacit Dimension*, London: Routledge & Kegan Paul.

Pólya, George (1945) *How to Solve it*, Princeton, NJ: Princeton University Press.

—— (1954) *Mathematics and Plausible Reasoning*, vols 1 (*Induction and Analogy in Mathematics*) and 2 (*Patterns of Plausible Inference*), London: Oxford University Press.

—— (1962) 'The Teaching of Mathematics and the Biogenetic Law' in I.J. Good (ed.) *The Scientist Speculates: An Anthology of Partly-Baked Ideas*, London: Heinemann, pp. 352–6.

Popper, Karl (1940) 'What is dialectic?', *Mind* 49, pp. 403–26.

—— (1957) *The Open Society and Its Enemies* (3rd edn), London: Routledge & Kegan Paul (1st edn 1945).

—— (1959) *The Logic of Scientific Discovery*, London: Hutchinson (first published in German as *Logik der Forschung*, 1934).

—— (1961) *The Poverty of Historicism* (3rd edn), London: Routledge & Kegan Paul (1st edn 1957).

—— (1963) *Conjectures and Refutations*, London: Routledge & Kegan Paul.

—— (1972) *Objective Knowledge: An Evolutionary Approach*, Oxford: Oxford University Press.

—— (1976) *Unended Quest*, London: Fontana.

Russell, Bertrand (1935) 'The Ancestry of Fascism' in *In Praise of Idleness*, London: George Unwin.

Sugar, P.F. (ed.) (1990) *A History of Hungary*, London: I.B. Tauris & Co.

Taylor, Charles M. (1975) *Hegel*, Cambridge: Cambridge University Press.

Wittgenstein, Ludwig (1958) *Philosophical Investigations* (2nd edn) (tr. G.E.M. Anscombe), Oxford: Blackwell (1st edn 1953).

—— (1978) *Remarks on the Foundations of Mathematics* (tr. G.E.M. Anscombe) G.H. Von Wright, R. Rhees and G.E.M. Anscombe (eds), Oxford: Blackwell.

Worrall, John (1985) 'Scientific Discovery and Theory–confirmation' in J.C. Pitt (ed.) *Change and Progress in Modern Science*, Dordrecht: Reidel.

Zinner, P.E. (ed.) (1956) *National Communism and Popular Revolt in Eastern Europe*, New York: Colombia University Press.

Index